TERRORISM: The SOVIET CONNECTION

Ray S. Cline & Yonah Alexander

Crane Russak / New York

**Terrorism:
The Soviet Connection**

Published in the United States by

Crane, Russak & Company, Inc.
3 East 44th Street
New York, NY 10017

Copyright © 1984 Center for Strategic and International Studies
Georgetown University
1800 K Street NW
Washington, DC 20006

Library of Congress Cataloging in Publication Data

Cline, Ray S.
Terrorism : the Soviet connection.

"Published in cooperation with the Center for Strategic
and International Studies, Georgetown University."
Bibliography; p.
Includes index.
1. Communist strategy. 2. Terrorism. I. Alexander,
Yonah. II. Title.
HX518.S8C54 1983   303.6'25   83-23162
ISBN 0-8448-1471-7 (Pbk.)

Printed in the United States of America

Second Printing 1984
Third Printing 1984

4|11|85 jc

TERRORISM:
The
SOVIET
CONNECTION

Contents

About the Authors

Ray S. Cline is Senior Associate, Center for Strategic and International Studies, Georgetown University, and Professor of International Relations. Educated at Harvard University, Cline was Deputy Director for Intelligence for the Central Intelligence Agency (1962–1966). He has written numerous books and articles, including *Secrets, Spies, and Scholars* and *The CIA: Reality Versus Myth*.

Yonah Alexander is Professor and Director, The Institute for Studies in International Terrorism, State University of New York. He is also a member of the senior research staff, Center for Strategic and International Studies, Georgetown University. Educated at Columbia University and the University of Chicago, Alexander is Editor of *Terrorism: An International Journal* and *Political Communication and Persuasion: An International Journal*. He has authored, edited, and co-edited 22 books.

Preface

As this volume was in preparation, an incident revealed in starkest terms the clash of two very different cultures, Soviet and American, on the propriety of resort to violence. A political and ethical gulf was never more clearly delineated than in the world reaction to the deliberate Soviet shooting down of a Korean airliner with 269 civilians aboard, including 61 Americans, at 0326 Korean time on September 1, 1983. The regularly scheduled passenger aircraft had strayed off course and passed through Soviet airspace over Kamchatka Peninsula and then over Sakhalin Island. The Korean pilot, apparently unaware of any navigational error, reported to Tokyo at 0323 Korean time that he was on the planned track northeast of Hokkaido, Japan.

After more than two hours of radar tracking of this aircraft and a near approach to it by a Soviet interceptor aircraft from Sakhalin, Soviet authorities gave instructions to fire a missile at the Korean plane as it was leaving Sakhalin and approaching the Sea of Japan. According to intercepted voice transmissions, the Soviet pilot reported at 0326 Korean time, "The target is destroyed. I am breaking off attack." The aircraft disappeared from radar screens at 16,000 feet altitude three minutes later. Everyone aboard was killed in the plane's plunge to the sea.

Despite the reaction of horror from the United States and most of the rest of the world, the Soviet Union has refused to recognize any error in this destruction of innocent human lives, because the aircraft had crossed the "sacred borders" of Soviet territory.

This concept of the political rights of the state overriding human life portends more and more politically inspired violence of the kind Americans find hard to believe. Revolutionary violence and guerrilla wars have spread to every continent in the past decade, just as a close reading of Soviet doctrinal literature indicates Moscow had planned. Not only protection of the "sacred borders" of the Soviet Union is involved, but also penetration of other nations' borders by Soviet revolutionary activists, guerrilla warriors, and professional terrorists. To the Kremlin's leaders, violence is justified not only defensively but also to support offensive political "liberation" moves.

The persistent strategic pattern of international destabilization and terrorism, assisted by if not always controlled from Moscow, has escaped the attention of the majority of U.S. observers. The news media search endlessly for the "smoking gun" of Soviet involvement, overlooking the fact that international training of revolutionary activists is a clandestine business in which fingerprints are concealed and complicity denied. Circumstantial evidence and the logical framework of doctrinal cause and revolutionary effect are all there is to go on in examining the case of the Soviet connection with the current global disorder.

A quantum jump in availability of evidence occurred in 1982 when documents captured in Lebanon illuminated the scope of Soviet use of the Palestine Liberation Organization (PLO) as a vehicle for destabilizing the Mideast and exporting terrorism worldwide.

My colleague and co-author, Professor Yonah Alexander, capitalized on the knowledge and contacts he has acquired during a lifelong career of research, writing, and teaching about terrorism to move quickly into Lebanon and gather fresh data on the Soviet-PLO connection. Combined with earlier material from many different regions, the 1982 documents cast a new light on the strategic dimensions and operational infrastructure of Soviet links with international violence and low-intensity warfare.

Guns galore there are, smoking or not, and the total framework of Soviet support of international terrorism is surely beyond reasonable questioning in view of all the information presented in this small volume. We have attempted to provide a badly needed public account of a systematic political and moral challenge to the way of life in the United States and other pluralist societies. In my opinion, nothing quite so informative is available outside the restricted intelligence files of governments, and perhaps not even there.

This publication has been literally put together from much raw data and many rough manuscripts in a tremendous editorial performance by Marjorie W. Cline. Dr. Alexander has requested that I acknowledge her indispensable contribution to the completion of this volume, and I am happy to do so because of my own appreciation of her diligence and skill in the perplexing problems of presenting such an avalanche of complex data in a rational manner. She deserves at least as much credit as the two authors for whatever value this analysis of the Soviet connection with terrorism may have.

Ray S. Cline
Senior Associate, CSIS
Director, World Power Studies Program

September 15, 1983

Chapter 1

Terrorism: The Strategic Dimension

As 1984 begins, the year George Orwell long ago made synony-
mous with political oppression, the odds increase in favor of
Soviet-sponsored revolutionary warfare and spectacular terrorist incidents, many of the latter involving Americans. As the
result of incessant drumfire of hostile propaganda against the
United States over many years, Americans are the primary
targets of terrorism in most foreign countries, particularly in
regions destabilized by revolutionary violence. And the United
States is not immune from such attacks within its own borders.

Imagine what might occur on a quiet Christmas Eve in 1984 if
some one hundred highly trained FALN Puerto Rican saboteurs
succeeded in penetrating the perimeter of a number of U.S.
military installations in the United States and Puerto Rico. High
explosives placed at preselected locations destroy an army ammunition depot, a naval communications station, barracks at a
Marine Corps training facility, and a petroleum products storage
annex. Repairing the damage to these facilities, amounting to
tens of millions of dollars, will require at least one year.

In Washington, D.C., at the same time, a special hit squad
operating from a moving vehicle on Massachusetts Avenue
launches a rocket projectile over the fence at Vice President
George Bush's official residence in the Naval Observatory com-
pound, blowing a huge hole in the back wall. Nobody is injured,
and the terrorists are not apprehended.

Shortly after dawn, anonymous callers to the *Washington
Post* instruct reporters where to search for a FALN communiqué, discovered a short time afterward at the Lincoln Memo-
rial. It reads as follows:

Last night our brave FALN commando unit attacked major Yankee
military facilities in occupied Puerto Rico and at many points within

1

the home territory of the United States. We consider this to be the most daring joint operation of freedom fighters ever undertaken against Yankee colonial domination.

The Christmas raid, along with other actions of the courageous FALN soldiers, underscores the seriousness of our demands for the prompt release of all Puerto Rican political prisoners in capitalist jails and the immediate and unconditional independence of Puerto Rico. We will achieve national liberation no matter how high the price. We will continue to strike at the two fronts, one in Puerto Rico and the other in the United States.

If our humanitarian and just demands are not met, we will escalate our operations in the near future. No American official responsible for keeping our homeland in the exploiting clutch of capitalist imperialism is safe. Let George Bush and the other Wall Street lackeys beware!

At the year's end, the public outcry is tremendous—criticizing the inability of law enforcement authorities and the military to deal effectively with terrorism. Many voices insist that the United States should immediately grant Puerto Rican independence. Some suggest that the FALN is a respectable "freedom fighter" organization motivated only by poverty and social inequity in Puerto Rico. Other voices argue that Soviet and Cuban encouragement of the FALN is the real force that makes such attacks possible and that the U.S. government should go to the source. In the United Nations, the Soviet Union, Cuba, and other socialist and Third World nations call for a special session of the General Assembly to discuss the continued "occupation" of Puerto Rico by the U.S. "imperialists." Washington policy-making grinds to a halt in confusion and frustration.

This hypothetical but perfectly realistic scenario demonstrates the grim facts of life about the prevalence of terrorism today and its use as an expedient tactical and strategic tool in the political struggle for power within and among nations. It also points up the increasing lack of distinction between war and peace. As we begin the year 1984, Orwell's famous Newspeak dictum that "peace is war" assumes greater reality. It is essential for Americans to understand that this is the kind of world we are living in, and why.

The typical low-level or low-intensity conflict has both domestic and international components. Violence, involving sabotage, insurrection, coup d'état, and civil war, is common among groups competing for power and social benefits internally in many nations. Terrorism, guerrilla warfare, insurgency, and revolutionary war are part of the vocabulary of international violence. These terms are often used interchangeably. The most serious situations develop when the stability and welfare of nations are threatened by domestic revolutionary forces encouraged and supported outside the national borders.

Increased ideological and political antagonisms cross a critical dividing line when urban and rural-based insurgent forces undertake terrorist acts in order to pose an imminent threat to a nation's political and economic vitality. If such terrorist units receive training, arms and ammunition, money, and political guidance from safe sanctuaries outside their own nation, they can more readily succeed in threatening economic, social, and governmental stability. They are thereby engaged in the front line of an international war for political control of a national government and hence the resources and people of the nation. A nation supporting terrorist violence in another nation is engaged in low-intensity warfare in support of expansion of its own sphere of political influence.

There are no simplistic solutions for reducing vulnerability to such destabilizing acts of violence. Both terrorism and counterterrorism can result in devastating destruction, often coupled with public alienation from a government unable to protect the safety of its citizens. As the first phase in unconventional warfare, a successful act of terrorism tends to erect an invisible barrier of noncooperation between people and their goverment. It announces to a nation and to the world that war has been declared on the existing government by shadowy and dangerous opposition forces. Repeated acts of terrorism are likely to occur and reveal—to the people and to the international community—the government's impotence in stopping the attacks.

Using a strategy of selective violence, terrorists take advantage of secrecy and surprise to mount attacks on those who are hostile to their objectives. They can then place the blame on the government for its lack of efficiency, while they pose as champions of the victims. An unrestrained clash between the terrorists and the establishment can cause loss of faith in all public institutions and create new problems for society under the guise of attempting to solve existing ones.[1]

Thus, terrorism is a mode of irregular warfare that is "cheap to activate and costly to counter."[2] As a form of low-intensity political conflict below the threshold of clearly recognized military operations and commonly accepted laws of war, terrorism is becoming one of the most menacing methods of disrupting the fabric of civilized order in an open society.[3] Ideological and political groups—ranging from left-wing theorists who see what they call an evil post-imperial system of oppression, to religious reactionaries who oppose secularism—are able to conduct political warfare on the national level with direct and indirect support from outside the state. If they ultimately succeed in altering the domestic political system, they also alter the balance of power on an international scale. It appears in this era that nuclear missiles are less likely to determine the results of U.S.-Soviet conflicts than the use of small arms and explosives by terrorists in the Mideast, Africa, or Central America.

Terrorism against the Shah's regime in Iran dramatically demonstrated that low-intensity conflict can bring about major changes in the environment by destroying governments aligned with the United States. Moreover, the tragic takeover of the U.S. Embassy in Tehran and the protracted 444 days of crisis that followed illustrated that terrorism, with continuous media coverage, can become a devastating political weapon causing broad international ramifications from nation to nation. Frustration with the inability to free the American hostages resulted in the U.S. government's launching a military rescue operation for which it was not adequately prepared. Its failure further reduced U.S. prestige and credibility.

While these and similar acts of terrorism sanctioned by Mideast nations are generally recognized as dangerous, there is still a considerable dispute among experts about whether and to what extent terrorism is sponsored and controlled by the Soviet Union.

Many observers believe that Moscow's strategic thinking calls for the manipulation of terrorism as a suitable substitute for traditional warfare, which has become too expensive and is too hazardous to be waged on the battlefield except in special circumstances in close proximity to Soviet borders, as in Afghanistan. By overtly and covertly resorting to nonmilitary techniques, and by exploiting low-intensity operations around the world, the Soviet Union is able to continue its revolutionary efforts against democratic pluralism in the free world as well as to expand its own influence into a wider target area.

Apologists for Soviet foreign policy, on the other hand, are skeptical about direct and indirect Soviet control of terrorist groups. While admitting that Moscow approves of and gives some assistance to what it considers legitimate "liberation movements," or struggles of people for their independence, proponents of this view argue that the dynamics of modern terrorism are so uncontrollable as to make the Soviet leaders ambivalent about the usefulness of this form of warfare.

In any case, the most important fact is that, whether or not Moscow controls terrorist and guerrilla warfare operations, the Soviet Union does continue to supply massive amounts of arms and money to the revolutionary forces involved. However, the scope and nature of Soviet involvement in terrorist activity is still obscure in the minds of many observers because it is fundamentally a secret or covert action program, ranging from the political legitimization of violence by propaganda to the supply of funds, training, arms, and other operational assistance. The Soviet role in these activities has fluctuated over the years and from place to place in accordance with Moscow's changing appreciation of its vital interests in different parts of the world. Specific terrorist operations have sometimes seemed to be no more than the coincidental by-product of Soviet propaganda and militant behavior.

While it is not always easy to determine whether a particular terrorist action or series of actions in any targeted country is homegrown or Moscow-inspired, the pattern of Soviet sponsorship of violence in many different regional conflicts is becoming clearer and clearer. In the past decade, the Soviet Union's position as an undisputed superpower has permitted it to control or strongly influence the foreign policy and international conduct of other socialist countries that subscribe to the Soviet ideological line.

In this context, Bulgaria, Cuba, Czechoslovakia, East Germany, North Korea, and Vietnam act as Soviet surrogates in exporting violence. The support provided by these countries to various Communist and non-Communist terrorist movements in both developed and developing nations is generally attributed to the decisionmakers in the Kremlin. This is because support could not be given without the knowledge and at least tacit approval of Soviet officials in the surrogate nations. Moscow-oriented socialist states, then, serve both as intermediaries between the Soviet Union and terrorists and as essential actors in assisting, or aiding and abetting, the promotion of ideological and political violence throughout the world.[4]

In the 1970s terrorism, whether backed directly or indirectly by the Soviet Union or independently initiated, appeared to have become an indispensable tactical and strategic tool in the Soviet struggles for power and influence within and among nations. In relying on this instrument, Moscow seems to aim, in the 1980s, at achieving strategic ends in circumstances where the use of conventional armed forces is deemed inappropriate, ineffective, too risky, or too difficult.

The broad goals the Soviet Union hopes to achieve from terrorism include the following:

1. *Influencing developments in neighboring countries.* Moscow planted subversive Communist seeds in Iran for decades, contributed by proxy to the fall of the pro-Western Shah, and is currently helping local Marxist-Leninist factions in Iran to try to establish the requisite conditions for the subsequent overthrow of the revolutionary Islamic government.
2. *Regaining irredentist territories in the Soviet orbit.* Moscow's goals in relation to Turkey are not only to undermine NATO's southern flank but also to incorporate portions of eastern Turkey (e.g., Kars and Ardahan) in the Soviet Union because of their strategic significance and geopolitical relationship to neighboring ethnic minorities in western Iran.

3. *Helping to create new states in which it will have considerable influence as a result of its support of those nations' claims for self-determination.* Soviet assistance to the Palestine Liberation Organization (PLO) is aimed at achieving this end.

4. *Weakening the political, economic, and military infrastructure of anti-Soviet alliances such as NATO.* A case in point is indirect Soviet support of the Irish Republican Army (IRA). Moscow hopes that if violence in Ulster continues, the United Kingdom, a member of NATO, will be neutralized as a potential adversary. The Euromissile demonstrations in Germany and other parts of Europe are in the propaganda phase, but they may end in more violent anti-NATO gestures.

5. *Initiating proxy operations in distant geographic locations where direct organized conventional military activities are logistically impracticable.* The Kremlin's manipulation of the South-West Africa People's Organization (SWAPO), based in Angola under Cuban troop protection, is aimed at setting up a Marxist regime with a pro-Soviet orientation in Namibia (South-West Africa) and thus gaining vital strategic and economic advantages in this region, with South Africa as the ultimate target for destabilization.

6. *Stirring up trouble for the United States in the highly visible region of Central America, particularly where such a policy entails no serious financial burden and is politically low-risk because of the use of surrogates like Cuba and Nicaragua.* The campaign of terrorism and guerrilla insurgency being fought in El Salvador—with support from Havana and Managua as well as Moscow—is a potential threat to the stability of the Caribbean, including Mexico. This is an area of great strategic importance as well as close proximity to the United States.

7. *Waging a "secret war" against individuals considered by the Kremlin as "mortal enemies" of Communism and the Soviet Union.* From the 1940 murder of Leon Trotsky in Mexico by Stalin's agents, to the circumstantial evidence linking Moscow through Bulgaria to the attempted assassination of Pope John Paul II, countless political assassinations have occurred

in situations where only the Soviet Union appeared likely to benefit.

Unless Americans become more conscious of the broad strategic dangers implicit in the patterns of contemporary terrorism and become more skillful in deterring or countering terrorist operations, the next two decades in this century will be catastrophic for worldwide security interests of the United States and its friends and allies abroad. This subtle assault on the values and defensive strengths of our society is not well understood, and its strategic implications for liberal democracies are only beginning to be explored.

Chapter 2

Soviet Ideologies and Policies

The roots of Soviet commitment to revolutionary violence go very deep and are enshrined in the doctrinal literature passed on systematically to successive generations of Communist Party leadership long before the current crises in Lebanon and Central America. The historical evidence indicates that the term "terrorist" was first adopted by a major revolutionary group in nineteenth-century Russia "as a badge of pride."[1] Indeed, similarly, Russia's justification for the use of terrorism as a legitimate political tool has its ideological roots in the works of the founders of orthodox Marxism-Leninism and prominent Communist writers. To a greater and lesser extent, the founders all advocated employing confrontation tactics—including terrorism—for achieving Communist aims.

In *Das Kapital* Karl Marx asserted: "Force *(Gewalt)* is the midwife of an old society which is pregnant with a new one."[2] Writing in 1848, Marx expressed a strong belief in the necessity of political violence: "Only one means exists to shorten the bloody death pangs of the old society and the birth pangs of the new society, to simplify and concentrate them—revolutionary terrorism."[3] It was therefore natural for Marx to criticize the French Communards of the early 1870s for failing to utilize terror, observing that "violence in itself is an economic [form of] power."[4]

This doctrine persisted not only in Marx's other writings but also with some modifications in the works of Lenin. Lenin too held that the revolutionary struggle might appropriately include terror. Writing in 1906, Lenin responded to critics of this approach by asserting that "no Marxist should consider partisan warfare (including political assassination) . . . as abnormal and demoralizing."[5] On the contrary, "terrorist partisan acts against representatives of the violent regime, are recommended."[6] That

9

is, terrorism was regarded by Lenin as a part of the "proletarian revolution," although he wanted it to be employed only under the direction of "the Party" and only where conditions existed for its success. It is not surprising, therefore, that he saw the usefulness of terrorism as a tactic of disorganization of the czarist enemy and as a means of acquiring experience and military training. On the other hand, Lenin condemned "individual," "infantile," or "isolated" political violence.

In short, Lenin proposed and substantiated a guideline aimed at creating a united front from all anti-imperialist forces in nations fighting for liberation from colonial and semi-colonial oppression.[7] The goal always is destabilization in preparation for revolution and Communist political rule.

Leon Trotsky unequivocally justified the resort to terrorism as a tactical tool of partisan warfare. He observed that this instrument can be very efficient against a reactionary class which does not want to leave the scene of operations, because it kills individuals and intimidates thousands.[8] While Trotsky was jettisoned by Stalin, his pragmatic endorsement of terror as an instrument of revolution remains embedded in Communist Party doctrine.

Nikita Khrushchev, once he had worked his way into power after Stalin's death in 1953, advanced Communist thinking beyond the concepts of his predecessors. The advent of the hydrogen bomb convinced Communist leaders that prudence required abandonment of Lenin's 1919 prediction that the Soviet Union and the Communist system would inevitably "triumph in the end" after a "frightful collision" with the capitalist states. The prospect of inevitable nuclear war was not attractive, so the Communist ideologues arrived at new formulations, sanctified by Khrushchev at the 20th Party Congress in February 1956.

The new doctrine, enshrined in the pronouncements of international Communist conclaves in 1957 and 1960, declared that war was "not inevitable." Instead, Communist victory would come as a result of unrelenting "class struggle" in capitalist nations and worldwide Soviet support of every "just war" of "national liberation." Thus eventually the Soviet Union would triumph without the "frightful collision" of a nuclear war as a consequence of the gradual spread of Communist strength from region to region causing a "disintegration of the world market" and a "general crisis in the world capitalist system," as predicted by Stalin.[9]

Thus capitalism or imperialism, as Soviet ideologues always term the United States and its international trading partners, would be destroyed not by frontal assault but from the economic rear. A succession of major victories in regional "liberation" conflicts would in time change the balance of power irreversibly, presaging Communist "triumph in the end."

In his report to Higher Party Schools attached to the Central Committee of the Soviet Communist Party on January 6, 1961, Khrushchev summarized the view that nuclear war with the United States was virtually unthinkable. Khrushchev suggested that instead there would be ample opportunity to undermine the stability of pro-Western regimes in Third World nations, especially those rich in minerals crucial to the industrial West, by training and arming underground Communist cadres for sabotage, guerrilla warfare, and terrorism. The immediate aim would be to weaken capitalism.

Khrushchev emphasized that the Soviet Union would prepare these forces for wars of national liberation, which he said were not only "admissible but inevitable." He later defended this speech to President John F. Kennedy, who had read it, when the two leaders met in Vienna. Khrushchev told Kennedy that these kinds of war were "sacred" and that the Soviet Union would certainly support them. From these doctrinal concepts, still enshrined in Soviet ideology today, most of the regional conflicts of the 1980s arise.

Two days after President Kennedy was inaugurated, on January 22, 1961, Khrushchev had already revealed his optimism about the triumph of socialism over capitalism.[10] He cited the success of Fidel Castro in Cuba, of Ho Chi Minh in Vietnam, of the National Liberation Front (FLN) in Algeria, and of the radical nationalist Patrice Lumumba, Zaire's first Prime Minister and trained by the KGB, who had made inroads into the Belgian Congo. Khrushchev then declared, "The victory of Communism is no longer far off."[11]

Leonid Brezhnev, in his turn after succeeding Khrushchev in 1964, urged the continuing liquidation of Western civilization. Indeed, at the 25th Party Congress in February 1976, his mood was buoyant in the light of the final U.S. defeat in Vietnam. He said, "Our party supports and will continue to support peoples fighting for their freedom."

Furthermore, he added, "It is farthest from the Communists' mind to predict an 'automatic collapse' of capitalism. It still has considerable reserves. Yet the developments of recent years forcefully confirm that capitalism is a society without a future."

Five years later, in February 1981 at the 26th Party Congress, Brezhnev was still ideologically stern. Mentioning gains in Angola, Ethiopia, Mozambique, the People's Republic of Yemen, and Afghanistan, he committed Moscow to the "consolidation of the alliance between world socialism and the national-liberation movement."

This philosophical justification of violence as the way to Leninist victory provided the mold that shaped the world view and long leadership career of Yuri Andropov, present chief executive of the Soviet Communist Party and state.

From the first Marxist-Leninist revolution against czarism—when more than a thousand terrorist acts were perpetrated in Transcaucasia alone—to the present day, Moscow-oriented Communism has encouraged and assisted terrorist groups that follow a strict party line and are highly centralized. Terrorist movements with less party discipline and control, including the New Left, and even Trotskyists (working for the furtherance of international Communism but generally hostile to the Soviet Union) have also on occasion received some kind of support when it destabilized Soviet target societies. Moreover, from considerations of political expedience rather than ideological solidarity, a wide range of extremist groups—sectarian, nationalist, separatist, and anarchist—have frequently been supported by the Soviet Union.[12]

Many of these movements have adopted Marxist ideologies mainly as a flag of convenience. They reasoned that Marxism provides a model for revolution against the state, denies the legal authority of the government, establishes a successful historical example of revolution, grants a measure of respectable international status because the Soviet Union is universally dealt with as a superpower, offers a sense of affinity with other revolutionary movements, and guarantees some assurance of direct and indirect support by like-minded groups and other socialist states. With the adoption of a Marxist philosophy, however, most of these terrorist movements have fallen victim to internal ideological debate, division, and conflict, ending usually with the violent extremists dominant.

Notwithstanding such ideological differences, the Soviet Union does not hesitate to provide assistance to a multitude of groups, holding that social discord and political turmoil in "enemy" territory is likely to advance Moscow's cause. The Bolsheviks therefore created the Communist International (Comintern) in March 1919 to promote the "inevitable" proletarian victory. Although this organization was abolished during World War II, the Soviet constitution, revised in 1977, declares that the Soviet Union has an obligation to support "national liberation movements." The history of such support goes back a long way.

One of the earliest examples of Soviet involvement in terrorist activities is the training of foreign revolutionaries at Tashkent in 1920. Guerrillas from India trained there were assigned by Lenin himself to conduct a terrorist bombing campaign against the British on the subcontinent. Once London uncovered the plot, it protested to Moscow and the mission was aborted.[13]

The Soviet Union also planned to promote terrorism elsewhere. In 1922, Soviet agents in Rome met with Abdul Hamid Sa'id, leader of the Egyptian terrorist group Nasrat ul-Hakh (Victory of Right), to plot the murder of leading British personalities, including Lord Allenby.[14] Subsequently, Georgi Chicherin, the Soviet Foreign Minister, promised the group "anything you may require toward the attainment of your object."[15]

It is interesting that these anti-British incidents, coupled with other cases involving direct and indirect Soviet involvement in political violence—ranging from open support of Irish revolutionaries[16] to terrorist operations in Singapore[17]—figure prominently in London's decision to break off diplomatic relations with Moscow on May 26, 1927.[18] This setback did not, however, deter the Kremlin from continuing its support of terrorist operations in the British Empire, including Egypt, India, and Palestine.[19]

In the 1930s the Kremlin undertook other subversive activities aimed at advancing the cause of the Communist International:

- Moscow funded the National Social Party in Germany for the purpose of destabilizing the nation.[20]
- The Soviets encouraged the Basque Separatists and Catalan Nationalists in Spain and provided funds, training, and weapons to leftist factions in the Civil War.[21]
- Communist agents were linked to bandits attacking business targets in Nicaragua.[22]
- Argentinian and Brazilian insurgents were financed and trained by the Soviet Union.[23]

Moscow's Latin American experience resulted in another diplomatic break. Convinced that the Soviets had established Montevideo as the center for their subversive operations in the region, Uruguay cut off its relations with the Kremlin on December 27, 1935.[24] Once again, this incident, as well as subsequent accusations by various governments of direct and indirect Soviet involvement in terrorism, did not modify Moscow's behavioral pattern of "low-level" conflict during and after World War II.

Yet it would be a gross exaggeration to assert that most terrorist operations worldwide are Soviet-sponsored. As Lord Chalfont has observed, "I do not believe that the forces of international terrorism are centrally inspired or centrally controlled, but I do suggest that when it suits their purpose, the forces of international Communism will support terror groups throughout the world."[25]

It is equally true that practical considerations have dictated that Soviet policy toward terrorism must be adapted to changing circumstances. More specifically, Moscow has long recognized that it too is vulnerable to various forms of terrorism. In fact, as early as the 1920s, Russia was the object of terrorist attacks by White Guard émigrés who used neighboring countries as operational bases. Exercising its right of self-defense, the Soviet Union sent troops into Mongolia and China to liquidate these bands.[26] During the interwar period, Moscow supported various international efforts to eliminate certain kinds of terrorism, particularly armed attacks.[27]

More recently, as a superpower with political, diplomatic, economic, and military interests all over the world, Moscow has adopted a cautious and restrained public rhetorical stand. The activities of various terrorist groups, including some that proclaim Marxist revolution to be their objective, have even been condemned as "adventurism." The Soviet Union has also at times acted in concert with capitalist states in opposing subnational violence. For example, it supported the U.N. Declaration on Principles of International Law Concerning Friendly Relations and Cooperation Among States in accordance with the Charter of the United Nations, adopted by the General Assembly as Resolution 2625 (XXV) on October 24, 1970. This document asserts, among other things, that terrorist and other subversive activities organized and supported by one state against another are a form of unlawful use of force. Soviet propaganda denials of responsibility for terrorism often cite this U.N. resolution.

As a nation with dissidents who sometimes perceive aerial hijacking as the only means of escaping to the West, the Soviet Union also participated in the 1970 Hague Convention for the Suppression of Unlawful Seizure of Aircraft, and the 1971 Montreal Convention for the Suppression of Unlawful Acts Against the Safety of Civil Aviation. In addition, it has concluded bilateral agreements with Iran and Finland to provide for the return of hijackers to that state where the aircraft is registered.[28]

Clearly, the Soviet Union has attempted to achieve a balance between opposition, in principle, to terrorist activities—to which it is itself vulnerable—and support for terrorist operations that attempt to tear down the fabric of Western society and weaken other nonsocialist governments. For example, subtle psychopolitical encouragement of non-state violence was provided by the Kremlin when it frustrated efforts to obtain U.S.

backing for a comprehensive international convention for the prevention of terrorism. The Soviet Union stated that it opposed "acts of terrorism . . . such as the murder and kidnapping of foreign citizens and aerial hijacking"[29] and also the attempt by Western powers to give a broad interpretation to the term "international terrorism" to encompass what Moscow calls "national liberation movements."[30]

The discrepancy between the Soviet Union's anti-terrorist public stance and its actions is quite apparent. Moscow's support of ideological and political violence in the post-Khrushchev era, rhetoric notwithstanding, plainly expanded. Two major factors contributed to the Kremlin's determination to play a more active role.

First, the turbulent 1960s saw some surprising global developments:

- The failure of the rural guerrilla movements in Latin America and the resort to urban guerrilla warfare and terrorism
- The defeat of the Arabs in the June 1967 war and the subsequent rise of Palestinian terrorism
- The Vietnam war and the widespread demonstrations against U.S. involvement in the war
- The French students' revolt in 1968

Second, many subnational movements adopted a certain comradeship in their struggle against imperialism, capitalism, and "international Zionism," for the liberation of dependent peoples.[31]

As Ulrike Meinhof, leader of West Germany's viciously violent Baader-Meinhof Gang, puts it in her manifesto, "We must learn from the revolutionary movements of the world—the Vietcong, the Palestine Liberation Front, the Tupamaros, the Black Panthers."[32]

Capitalizing on these welcome developments on the world scene, Moscow became intimately involved with a substantial number of terrorist groups, however misguided their operations might be. Of course, as a respected member of the "family of nations," the Kremlin could not openly support these movements lest they jeopardize its peaceful relations with various nations. The policy of détente, which brought the Soviet Union considerable benefits, also dictates clandestine methods of assisting terrorist activities.

Yuri Andropov, newly elected General Secretary of the Central Committee of the Communist Party of the Soviet Union, announced his commitment to the Soviet role in national liberation movements in a speech delivered at the funeral of Brezhnev on November 15, 1982:

> We will do our utmost to strengthen further the cohesion of the great community of socialist states, the unity of the world's Communists in the struggle for their common goals and ideals. We will maintain and develop our solidarity and our cooperation with the countries which have thrown off the colonial yoke, with the peoples struggling for their national independence and social progress.[33]

Again on December 21, 1982, Andropov vowed Moscow's support for worldwide liberation movements:

> The Soviet Union's active and determined struggle for the abolition of colonialism, its unfailing support for the cause of liberation and equality of nations, facilitate their advance towards freedom and progress. This is well known to the peoples of Asia and Africa, the Arab East and Latin America.[34]

Chapter 3

Charges and Countercharges

There was a vast proliferation of violence in the 1970s, much of it generated by local social and economic problems that would cause trouble whether the Soviet Union intervened or not. Statistics indicate the trend continues upward.

In 1982 the U.S. Department of State recorded 746 international incidents involving terrorism conducted with the support of a foreign government or organization against foreign nationals, institutions, or governments. A total of 117 groups operating in 93 countries claimed credit for the incidents. More than one-fourth of their actions took place in three nations, 50 in France, 52 in Italy, and 108 in West Germany.

Moreover, U.S. citizens suffered from 385 of these attacks—more than one-half—of the 746 total.[1]

If the Kremlin designated any of these conflicts as revolutionary or liberation wars, outside support and tactical directions were automatically provided from Moscow or from subordinate Communist revolutionary headquarters in places like Damascus, Havana, or Hanoi. Then the conflicts escalated into low-intensity warfare.

Political observers and media reporters, unfamiliar with Soviet doctrine and global strategic concepts, are naturally confused and misled by deliberate Soviet semantic ambiguity about the Soviet connection with terrorism. Propaganda citing "peace struggles" and "freedom fighters" obscures the role Soviet political encouragement, weapons, and money inevitably play in destabilizing societies in the regions in which the "liberation" wars take place. Soviet assistance is usually covert or indirect, hence plausibly deniable and usually officially denied.

Evidence of international terrorist intervention, while circumstantial and plentiful, is naturally too scrappy, vague, and unconvincingly sourced to hold up in a court of law or even definitively in a court of world opinion. The voluminous record of local, little-read newspapers and particularly the vast archives of PLO documents captured in Lebanon in 1982 offer overwhelming proof of Soviet direct ties to the PLO and their terrorist training camps. The documents and newspaper data are fragmentary, but in their entirety they are virtually irrefutable and totally damning. Yet the information is not easily acquired and little noted.

The revolutionaries more often than not win in the battle of propaganda charges and countercharges. Truth is one of the first victims in a war of national liberation. It is a grave handicap for the government in an open society like the United States, laboring under such a disadvantage in identifying its adversaries as well as its own goals.

Countering the spread of destabilizing violence and Soviet influence is a strategic must for the United States, although the record is uneven and ambivalent as far as congressional and media opinion is concerned. The meaning of the PLO role as revealed by the Lebanon documents needs to be more fully understood.

U.S. Charges

In a clear departure from previous administrations, the Reagan administration has focused its attention on the question of ideological and political violence, especially direct and indirect Soviet involvement in terrorism. This U.S. policy has caused a surge of semantic evasions of responsibility for terrorism by Soviet spokesmen and a furious counterattack.

In numerous messages to the Kremlin, the President, the Secretary of State, and other U.S. officials have signaled that the United States is unwilling any longer to play by Moscow's rules governing Soviet-U.S. relations. Under the rules of the 1970s, the Soviet Union enjoyed the benefits of coexistence and détente—or relaxed tension—with the United States. At the same time, the Soviet Union remained free to promote "national liberation movements."

At his confirmation hearings on January 14, 1981, Secretary of State Designate Alexander Haig, himself a victim of a 1979 assassination attempt during his tenure as NATO commander, told the Senate Foreign Relations Committee that the Soviets are "training, funding, manning, and equipping the so-called forces of liberation or terrorist forces throughout the world."[2]

This emphasis on terrorism and the central role played by the Soviet Union has continued ever since. In welcoming the released American hostages back from their Iranian captivity on January 27, President Ronald Reagan warned, "Let terrorists be aware that when the rules of international behavior are violated, our policy will be one of swift and effective retribution."[3]

During his press conference the following day, Secretary Haig proclaimed, "International terrorism will take the place of human rights in our concern because it is the ultimate abuse of human rights." He also charged that "Moscow continues to support terrorism and war by proxy with a conscious policy— programs, if you will, which foster, support, and expand international terrorism." Haig concluded, "When you get to the bottom line, it is the Soviet Union which bears a major responsibility today for the proliferation and the hemorrhaging of international terrorism as we've come to know it."[4]

Elaborating on these assertions, a State Department spokesman listed examples of Soviet backing. Evidence included:

- Financial support, training, and arms given to groups such as the PLO
- Surrogate use of Cubans and Libyans to assist terrorist organizations
- Moscow's propaganda effort aimed at energizing national liberation movements
- Propaganda supportive of the hostage-taking of Americans in Iran
- General Soviet advocacy of armed struggle as a solution to regional problems, such as in El Salvador and Namibia, promoting the use of terrorism and impeding the peaceful resolution of conflicts

He also added that if Moscow "clearly understands that their fostering of terrorism is going to be very important to our future relations, then I think the [Soviets] will take heed."[5]

In February 1981 the U.S. Department of State issued a White Paper citing definitive evidence of support given to the Salvadoran rebels in late 1979 and early 1980, immediately after the Communist takeover in Nicaragua, by the Soviet Union, Cuba, East Germany, and their allies. "In short, over the past year," the paper revealed, "the insurgency in El Salvador has been progressively transformed into a textbook case of indirect armed aggression by Communist powers through Cuba." The evidence, drawn from captured guerrilla documents and war matériel and corroborated with intelligence reports, leaves no doubt that the Communist role was to provide direct and decisive support to Marxist factions in their effort to install a Communist regime against the will of the Salvadoran people.

Soviet Countercharges

It is not surprising that the White Paper provoked an immediate and sharp response from Moscow. When in February 1981 President Brezhnev addressed the issue in his speech to the 26th Party Congress, he deplored the "aggressiveness of the policy of imperialism, above all American" and hailed "the glory of the Communists, courageous fighters for the cause of the people."

Again, at the Czechoslovak Party Congress on April 7, Brezhnev referred to "unacceptable demands" that Moscow "cease rendering support to its friends" in Third World countries. And on April 27, in welcoming Libya's Colonel Mu'ammar el-Qaddafi to Moscow as a "comrade in the struggle for the rights and freedoms of peoples," Brezhnev repudiated the views of the United States by saying, "Imperialists have no regard either for the will of the people or the laws of history. Liberation struggles cause their indignation. They describe it as 'terrorism.'"[6]

Similarly, Marshal Dimitri Ustinov, member of the Politburo of the Soviet Communist Party and Minister of Defense, defined terrorism as the actions of "neo-fascism," excluding by definition the "progressive actions" of "national liberation struggle." He further pointed out that the "evil-minded" charges against Moscow were intended "to cover up Western subversion of Poland and other countries." In general, Ustinov concluded, terrorism is "one of the most terrible manifestations of the moral and political crisis of capitalist society and the embodiment of lawlessness."[7]

First Deputy Minister of Justice of the Soviet Union, Aleksandr Sukharev, accused the Central Intelligence Agency (CIA) of direct or indirect involvement in the murder of Patrice Lumumba, Prime Minister of the Republic of Zaire, in 1960; of Amilcar Cabral, General Secretary of the African Party of Independence of Guinea and Cape Verde Islands, in 1973; of Salvador Allende, President of the Republic of Chile, in 1973; and of Brigadier General Omar Torrijos, President of the Republic of Panama, in 1981.[8]

Supplementing the statements by the Kremlin's leadership, the Soviet media, ranging from *TASS* to foreign broadcasting services, have conducted an intensive propaganda campaign aimed at audiences at home and abroad. The monothematic message, repeated continuously, is that it is the United States and not the Soviet Union that is principally responsible for encouraging low-level conflict and promoting international chaos through terrorism, sabotage, and subversion. More specifically, the Soviet media has made six broad assertions in support of this message:

1. The United States is dishonest when it equates "terrorism and the legitimate struggle of the peoples for their national, economic, and social emancipation. It is only through ignorance or by evil design that one can draw a parallel between these two absolutely different things."[9]
2. "The Soviet Union has always been and remains a principled opponent of the theory and practice of terrorism, including terrorism in international relations. Terrorism is organically alien to the world outlook of the Soviet people, to the policy of the Soviet state."[10]
3. Moscow pledges "to adhere to the well-known principles of recognizing the right of every people to resolve their own internal affairs without external interference." The Soviet international revolutionary vanguard will prevail in production

sharing and technological cooperation to further consolidate the alliance between world socialism and national liberation movements.[11]

4. The allegations of the United States concerning Moscow's direction of international terrorist operations is merely a myth to replace Washington's previous myth of working to secure human rights throughout the world.[12] The United States "has so far failed to ratify such agreements as the U.N. Convention on the Prevention and Punishment of the Crime of Genocide; the International Covenant on Civil and Political Rights; the International Covenant on Economic, Social, and Cultural Rights of 1966; and the International Convention on the Suppression and Punishment of the Crimes of Apartheid of 1973. Of nineteen U.N. treaties dealing exclusively with human rights, Washington has ratified only five."[13]

5. "Terrorism is a constant, immutable element in U.S. foreign policy" designed to "ideologically justify the escalation of American 'aggressiveness' particularly aimed at undermining the right of nations to self-determination."[14]

6. "U.S. criminal circles" and "the gentlemen at Langley" are not only systematically engaged in clandestine activities in the Third World but are also jeopardizing détente, destabilizing the political structure of the "Socialist Community," and even threatening civil liberties within the United States as well.[15] Moreover, the recent "reorganization of the CIA means a dramatic increase in America's terroristic elements: murders, conspiracies, subversion, and all the things which have now become for the American people themselves a repellent burden in practical as well as moral terms."[16]

Indeed, the Soviet media have seized every opportunity to reinforce these general allegations with specific cases. The following examples, selected at random, illustrate how Moscow has described U.S. "terrorist" efforts:

- Use of "propaganda campaign" in Poland to create chaos[17]
- "Propaganda war" against Vietnam, Laos, and Kampuchea[18]
- "Undeclared war" against Afghanistan and Iran[19]

- "Special attachment to dictatorial anti-popular regimes" in Chile and Paraguay[20]
- Military assistance to the government of El Salvador and to the rebels in Angola[21]
- Coups d'état in Chile, Cyprus, and the Seychelles[22]
- A "CIA conspiracy against Sandinistas"[23]
- Manipulation of "both left-wing and right-wing terrorist networks in Italy"[24]
- CIA backing "terrorist acts against Yugoslav institutions in Europe and the United States"[25]
- Training of terrorist groups in Germany and Egypt for operations in Iran[26]
- Creation in the United States of several military camps where a foreign legion of emigrants, intended for "struggle against the Reds," is being trained and organized, and whose purpose is to infiltrate Cuba, Nicaragua, and Poland[27]
- Financing and arming of Israeli "terrorists" and Afghan "bandits"[28]
- Bombing of the Islamic Republican headquarters in Tehran and employing of the Forgan "terrorist" organization and the Amal "counterrevolutionaries" to "disrupt the Iranian political system"[29]
- Kidnapping leaders of Paraguay's Communist Party (PCP) by U.S. "agents"[30]
- Plotting to assassinate Bangladesh President Ziaur Rahman, Cuba's Fidel Castro, Grenada's leader Maurice Bishop, and Zambian head of state Kenneth Kaunda[31]
- Murdering Afghanistan's General Fateh Mohammad Fermaershi, Bangladesh President Mujibur Rahman, Chile's Salvador Allende, Ayatollah A. Madani (Khomeini's aide), and high-ranking military officers in Iran[32]
- Sheltering hijackers of Soviet airliners[33]
- Encouragement of groups such as "the notorious Jewish Defense League" to undertake terrorist attacks against Soviet diplomats in New York[34]
- Direct U.S. involvement in Italian terrorism, as illustrated by the CIA link with the right-wing P-2 Masonic Lodge[35]

Radio Moscow, TASS, Pravda, and *Izvestia* have been and continue to be the most active in conducting a worldwide campaign to spread Soviet misinformation about the United States. In addition to U.S. imperialists, in general, the most popular targets are the CIA and the U.S. embassies abroad.

- On February 23, 1982, *Radio Moscow* alleged, "many people in America wonder whether the Dozier case was not from start to finish a provocation by the CIA. . . . Such an operation could have been prepared to direct public attention away from the Pentagon's dangerous plans in Western Europe and to reduce the intensity of the antiwar movement in NATO countries."
- Also in February 1982 *Radio Moscow* claimed the CIA was kidnapping children of Salvadoran refugees in Honduras. The poor peasants, the report went on to say, could only acquiesce since their children were threatened with death by starvation.
- On July 24, 1982, *TASS* reported that the CIA and the Pentagon had formed special forces with Green Berets. Their targets in clandestine operations are, above all, the socialist nations and nations of socialist orientation.
- In Zimbabwe on July 26, 1982, *TASS* reported that unidentified terrorists attacked the Thornhill air base. Unconfirmed television data stated that twelve combat aircraft were damaged. The news agency reported that it believes the operation was carried out by racist-ruled South Africa and the CIA to destabilize the Zimbabwe situation.
- On November 5, 1982, *Pravda* published another article about the CIA in Honduras, stating that the agency was working with the Pentagon "trying to use counterrevolutionary rabble and mercenaries to stifle revolution."
- An assertion made by *TASS* on February 1, 1983, said, "The Honduran army is to be the U.S. 'main gendarme in Central America'" and "Somozaist gangs" trained and armed by the CIA are mounting operations against Nicaragua.
- Perhaps the most serious development in Soviet misinformation on Afghanistan during November and December 1982 accused the U.S. Embassy in Kabul of "directing the hand of

murderers, agent saboteurs, and brutal bandits." *Izvestia,* the source of this story, claimed that these activities "have aroused just wrath and indignation among the Afghan public."

- In a *Radio Moscow* broadcast of February 11, 1983, Aleksandr Timoshkin charged that "U.S. imperialists could be considered the ones who taught the Zionists to kill Arabs and who trained the executioners." Timoshkin went on to say that U.S. imperialism had "vast and bloody experience" and its "wars of annihilation" against Korea, Vietnam, Kampuchea, and Afghanistan. Furthermore, he stated that U.S. imperialists "shared responsibility with Tel Aviv and Zionism for the crimes of the latter at Sabra and Shatila."

In more general terms, Soviet writers expound on their perception of U.S. "terrorism." On January 24, 1983, *Pravda* reviewed *Bloody Traces of American Imperialism,* a full-length book containing several chapters by various authors dealing with the theory and practice of terrorist actions by the United States against peoples fighting for freedom and independence. Washington's hegemonic course, in the authors' view, is shaped under the influence of the most reactionary, adventurous, and bellicose circles whose hatred of Communism is apparently stronger than common sense. The authors conclude that the "United States, by using terrorism and gruesome crimes, is trying to keep anti-people regimes in power with the help of its proxies" and to "suppress the peoples' struggle for liberation and social progress."[36]

In outlining the contents of two other books, *Pravda* notes further accusations against the United States. The most blatant in *Secret War Against Cuba* says Washington has a "pathological hatred of the freedom island" and that it has waged a secret war "at the will and under the guidance of all American administrations—from Kennedy to Reagan."[37] *Who Organizes and Directs International Terrorism* names the United States as the culprit "which turned terrorism into a tool of its policy from the beginning of the century."[38]

The U.S.-Soviet verbal confrontation on this subject was brought into focus when investigative reports in the U.S. media

contended that there was substantial circumstantial evidence
that linked the Soviet Union to the attempted assassination of
Pope John Paul II on May 13, 1981.[39] Although Washington
agreed that there was a strong suspicion that footprints of the
Soviet Security Agency (KGB) were in St. Peter's Square—
through the Bulgarian connection—it pointed out that there was
no smoking gun that proved Moscow's role.[40]

Notwithstanding this cautious U.S. official position, the
Soviet Union undertook an intensive propaganda response
aimed at refuting the speculation about Moscow's involvement
in the attempted assassination. Leonid M. Zamyatin, a member
of the Communist Party's Central Committee and Chief of the
International Information Department, called the speculation
"an evil-minded campaign that has not a grain nor an iota of
truth."[41] He further asserted that the accusation was initiated by
"right wing publications" in the West intended to discredit the
Soviets in the eyes of Roman Catholics throughout the world.

Similarly, the Soviet media denied any plot to kill the Pope.
TASS, for instance, asserted that the CIA was responsible for
"fabricating foul anti-Soviet sensations." It would have been
better to expose the CIA, *TASS* contended, suggesting that the
agency was behind the murder of such leaders as Orlando
Letelier, a former Allende minister.[42]

In a *Radio Moscow* broadcast in English on January 23, 1983,
TASS criticized U.S. Defense Secretary Caspar Weinberger for
suggesting that the charges against the KGB were "not entirely
groundless." Calling the Defense Secretary "a pathological liar,"
the radio commentators observed that "the remarkable thing is
that the mythical 'involvement' of Bulgaria and the Soviet Union
in 'international terrorism' is being alleged by those who are
giving support to the repressive regimes in Chile and El Salvador, backing the Israeli aggressors, engineering assassinations
of notable politicians and statesmen in other countries and regarding day-to-day violence in their own country as nothing out
of the ordinary."

On February 23, 1983, the *Moscow Domestic Service* com-
plained in Russian that Vice President George Bush during a
visit to Italy "tried to exert pressure on Italian officials to compel

them to produce proof of the socialist countries' involvement in the attempt to assassinate John Paul II." In another broadcast in Italian on the same day, *Radio Moscow* elaborated: "It emerges that the White House empowered the U.S. Vice President to inform the Italian leadership that President Reagan fully supported the activities of the Italian authorities as regards the inquiry into the attack on the Pope, even if this should negatively affect the Soviet-American negotiations in Geneva on the limitation of nuclear arms and lead to their failure."

Congressional Inquiry—Tentative Conclusions

The foregoing U.S.-Soviet exchanges sparked an intensive public debate in the United States as to whether and to what extent the Soviet Union has been involved in ideological and political violence. Officials of the State Department, the Justice Department, the Central Intelligence Agency (CIA), and other agencies concerned with the problem of domestic and international law were divided as to the nature of the Soviet role and the consequences. Some held to the administration's position; others challenged its validity.[43]

Possible Soviet sponsorship of terrorism became a subject of consideration on Capitol Hill, where Senator Jeremiah Denton's Subcommittee on Security and Terrorism of the Committee on the Judiciary has held hearings. Among the first witnesses to appear before the subcommittee during its first session on May 26, 1981, was Robert Moss, a journalist and author. Moss expressed his concern about the reluctance to study terrorism or Soviet involvement in this area of political violence. He asserted that four major reasons account for this reluctance: the dearth of evidence concerning Soviet terrorist activity; problems with defining just who the terrorists are; identifying Soviet involvement with that of its subcontractors; and the illusion that U.S. and Soviet leaders act under the same intellectual and moral orientations. He concluded that Americans must give up this illusion if they are to understand and to counter Soviet participation in terrorism.[44]

This and like-minded testimonies before the Subcommittee on

Security and Terrorism raise the question of how terrorism fits into Marxist ideology and Soviet behavior. In a statement issued on February 2, 1983, Senator Denton reported, "The hearings . . . documented extensive involvement and complicity by the Soviet Union and its surrogates in a worldwide network of terrorism, much of which takes place in the name of 'national liberation' movements." Elaborating on this involvement Senator Denton asserted, "The hearings demonstrated that Soviet exploitation of those movements included military and political training in the Soviet Union and its proxy states; furnishing equipment, including special weapons, money, documents, and escape mechanisms; furnishing advisers, some of whom participated in the selection of civilian targets; and furnishing propaganda support directly in the Soviet and satellite press as well as through stories planted in international press. The hearings also disclosed Soviet use of U.N. organizations to help promote and legitimize 'national liberation' organizations that employ terrorism to accomplish their goals."[45]

For the expert who reads congressional reports and other files of evidence, the pattern is clear, revealing Soviet strategic responsibility for some of the most troublesome conflicts and terrorist violence upsetting peace and security for millions of people. Unfortunately, the ordinary citizen seldom encounters the congressional findings as set forth above and accordingly suspends judgment on the cacophony of charges and countercharges.

This situation should change as the avalanche of comparatively hard evidence that has come to light in Lebanon concerning Soviet-PLO collaboration sinks into the public consciousness. As a case history, the PLO performance in the capacity of Soviet-manipulated external base and transmission belt for the export of revolutionary violence is more and more visible at the center of the turbulence of the past decade. Dissemination of these facts should mark a decisive phase in the battle to illuminate opinion on the character of international terrorism. The PLO story, at least, and the Soviet connection with PLO efforts to create a vast infrastructure for the export of terrorist activities, can no longer be brushed off by honest scholarly and news media commentators.

Chapter 4

The PLO Transmission Belt

The controversy over the exact dimensions of the Soviet role in furthering terrorism—or "national liberation," as it is called—will probably continue into the foreseeable future. The basic and seminal Soviet-PLO connection, however, is extremely well established by facts and documents recently uncovered in Lebanon.

Moscow's commitment to a visible linkage with the PLO is a result of the direct and indirect benefits it derives from exacerbating the Arab-Israeli conflict and destabilizing the once prosperous multicultural society and market economy of Lebanon. The PLO has also served as a transmission belt for the export of KGB terrorist techniques to other regions and hence constitutes an essential element in Soviet regional and global strategy.

The PLO, then, helps weaken and restrict U.S. ("imperialist") influence in the Mideast. As a major international guerrilla/terrorist movement, the PLO at the same time assists in transmitting doctrines and skills to promote destabilizing campaigns by other terrorist groups in Europe, Latin America, the Caribbean, Asia, and Africa.

Until 1969 the Kremlin paid little attention to the PLO, casting doubt on Palestinian effectiveness.[1] As a liberation movement it had its beginning in the early 1950s when Palestinian university students in the Arab countries, particularly in Syria and Lebanon, formed paramilitary youth groups and became active in Arab refugee camps. Although they sought to restore "Arab Palestine" to its "rightful owners," they failed to translate their theories into action. In fact, the proliferation of some fifty organizations in the next decade demonstrated their inability to unite against the common enemy.

Officially, the PLO and its military arm, the Palestine Liberation Army (PLA), were formed at the Arab-Cairo Summit in January 1964. Headquartered in Cairo, the PLO was organized by the Arab League to provide the military means for destroying Israel. Ahmed Shukairy, who headed the group, believed in the long-term development of a regular "liberation" force that would attack the Jewish state when it was properly prepared. His political mentor was President Gamal 'Abdul Nasser of Egypt, and his base of operations against the Jewish state was the Egyptian-ruled Gaza Strip.[2] Several months after the Israeli military victory in the June 1967 war, Shukairy, who was bitterly attacked by other Palestinian groups for the defeat, was forced to resign his position as Secretary-General. The PLO was plagued by internal strife following his departure and lost much of its earlier power. Since then, the history of the Palestinian movement has been characterized by separatism and fragile political amalgamation.[3]

The most important guerrilla organization that has survived the test of time, providing leadership and playing the role of a unifying force, is Harakat Tahrir Falastin (Movement for the Liberation of Palestine), better known as Fatah (Conquest). Formed in 1956 under Egyptian sponsorship, the group is led by Yasser Arafat, an engineer who developed the movement's ideology and strategy and went on to become the head of the PLO. Under Arafat's leadership, Fatah was able to appeal to the majority of the Palestinians—although they have never been given a choice of representation—and since 1970 it has become the major power center and dominant group within the PLO.[4]

In the aftermath of the war in Lebanon in the summer of 1982, Arafat's leadership was challenged by more extreme elements within the Fatah. Radical militants, led by Colonel Abu Musa and backed by Libya and Syria, rejected Arafat's use of diplomacy coupled with violence as an approach to the Arab-Israeli problem rather than unrelenting military attack. When Arafat ordered a cutoff of goods and supplies to the PLO militants in May 1983, they seized a Fatah warehouse near Damascus, with Syrian connivance. A bloody clash between the mutinous members and those loyal to Arafat followed the next month. The struggle is not yet over. The result will probably be greater Syrian (pro-Soviet) control and less flexibility in considering Mideast peace initiatives.

Regardless of how this intra-PLO conflict is resolved, it is unlikely that the organization as a whole will relinquish its commitment to the uncompromising Palestinian National Charter, which calls unequivocally for the elimination of Israel through "armed struggle." Adopted by the PLO's National Congress in 1968, the charter contains the following major principles:

Article 9: Armed struggle is the only way to liberate Palestine. Thus it is the overall strategy, not merely a tactical phase. . . .

Article 15: The liberation of Palestine, from an Arab viewpoint, is a national duty and it attempts to repel the Zionist and imperialist aggression against the Arab homeland and aims at the elimination of Zionism in Palestine.

Article 19: The partition of Palestine in 1947 and the establishment of the state of Israel are entirely illegal, regardless of the passage of time. . . .

Article 20: Judaism being a religion is not an independent nationality.

Article 21: The Arab Palestinian people, expressing themselves by the armed Palestinian revolution, reject all solutions which are substitutes for the total liberation of Palestine. . . .

Article 22: The liberation of Palestine will destroy the Zionist and imperialist presence and will contribute to peace in the Middle East. . . .

In 1968, Boris Ponomarev, head of the International Department of the Central Committee of the Soviet Communist Party, offered Soviet facilities for training guerrillas to Palestinian factions, and Ahmed Jibril, a Syrian army captain, inspected them. Then, intensive PLO terrorist operations in 1969 sparked Moscow's interest in the organization as a potential asset for assuring Soviet influence over events in the Mideast. In February, *TASS* praised the PLO's initial raids into Israel and called them wars of national liberation "conducted by patriots in defense of a legitimate right to return to their native land." In October of the same year, Aleksandr Shelepin, an official in the KGB, said, "We consider the struggle of the Palestine patriots for the liquidation of the consequences of Israeli aggression a just anti-imperialist struggle of national liberation and we support it."

Yet the Kremlin's initial support was limited. Arafat's visits to the Soviet Union were considered unofficial. The Soviets and their East European satellites provided only restricted training and military assistance, and Soviet leaders refused to open a PLO office in their capital.[5]

A dramatic change in the Kremlin's attitude toward the PLO occurred as a result of two major developments:

First, in the aftermath of the Israeli victory in the October 1973 war, the political position of the United States in the Mideast improved considerably.[6]

Second, the Rabat Arab Summit Conference in October 1974 recognized the PLO as "the sole legitimate representative of the Palestinian people."[7] These events led the Kremlin leadership to conclude that noncooperation with the PLO would exclude the Soviet Union from efforts to reach a settlement on the Arab-Israeli conflict. Once this conception crystallized in Moscow, the Soviets developed multilevel relations with the PLO. They established political and diplomatic relations as well as military linkages.

Political, Diplomatic, and Cultural Relations

The "Beirut-Moscow Axis," which was initiated during 1974, resulted in stronger ties between the Kremlin and the PLO. After Aleksandr A. Soldatov, formerly the Soviet Ambassador in Havana, was assigned as an envoy in Beirut, he met with Arafat on a regular basis—usually once a week—at the Soviet Embassy in order to coordinate major policies and military activities. For example, in a six-week period during 1982, Soldatov and Arafat had seven meetings. Arafat, as well as other PLO officials, including Farouk Kaddoumi, the PLO's unofficial foreign minister, met on many occasions with Soviet diplomats and dignitaries visiting Beirut.[8] Some two hundred meetings took place between the PLO, Soviet, and East European representatives. Frequent meetings were also held in Moscow.

In August 1974 the Soviet Union agreed to permit the PLO to set up a formal office in Moscow. The office opened in June 1976 and was granted embassy status in October 1981. Describing the nature of this development, Muhamed Al Sha'er, the PLO representative in Moscow, stated: "Relations between the PLO and Moscow couldn't be better, with both parties maintaining close political ties. The PLO has a coordination agreement with the Soviet Union. . . . The PLO enjoys special diplomatic status in ·the Soviet Union. The PLO representative is free to travel throughout the country, unlike other diplomatic representatives."[9]

Indeed, the PLO's Moscow office facilitated high-level meetings with the Soviet leadership—President Leonid Brezhnev, and Politburo members Alexei Kosygin, Mikhail Suslov, and Yuri Andropov, now the head of state. For example, in March 1978 Arafat met with Brezhnev and joined the Soviet leader in condemning President Anwar Sadat's participation in the peace process. Their joint communiqué made note of "the situation in the area as a result of the actions of the imperialists and Arab reactionism. . . ., the important role of the progressive forces of the Arab world, and the importance of uniting them with their natural allies—the USSR and the socialist countries."

One of the most unusual meetings was held in Moscow on November 13, 1979, at noon. Representing the Soviet Union were Andrei Gromyko, Foreign Minister; Boris Ponomarev, senior ideologue and international expert of the Soviet Communist Party's Central Committee apparatus; and Oleg A. Grinevsky, head of the Midcast Department of the Foreign Office. The PLO delegation included Yasser Arafat; Muhamed Al Sha'er, representing the PLO in Moscow; and delegates from Sa'iqa created by the Syrian Ba'ath Party in 1968, the Popular Front for the Liberation of Palestine (PFLP)* set up by George Habash in 1967, the Popular Front–General Command, an offshoot of the Habash group organized by Ahmed Jibril soon after the 1956 war over Nasser's seizure of the Suez Canal, the Democratic Front for the Liberation of Palestine (DFLP)† headed by Yassir Abed Rabah, the Arab Liberation Front under Abed El Rahim Ahmed, and the PLO Executive Committee.

The minutes of this meeting include a report by Arafat on Arab and Islamic summit meetings, and on PLO cooperation

*Hereafter referred to as the Popular Front (PFLP).
†Hereafter referred to as the Democratic Front (DFLP).

with the various Arab states—especially the members of the
"Steadfastness Front." Arafat condemned U.S. policy in the
Mideast by accusing the United States of trying to create splits
between Arab nations and of trying to impose the Camp David
autonomy program on the residents of the Israeli-occupied territories. Gromyko, in turn, outlined Soviet Mideast policy, particularly with respect to Lebanon. He praised PLO and Syrian
efforts to check the "American offensive" in that country and to
block U.S. attempts to "exploit" the Lebanese crisis. Ponomarev struck out against the United States. "Lately we established a committee for friendship and solidarity with the
Palestinian people. When the Vietnamese people struggled with
the U.S.A., we established a similar committee for solidarity,"
he said. "Vietnam, as we know, won later, and we hope that this
time victory will be achieved too."[10]

A few months later Arafat concluded an agreement with the
Soviets detailing bilateral coordination activities. As the PLO
representatives in the Soviet Union put it: "When a problem
arises, a high level delegation is sent by the PLO to Moscow for
discussion and for a common stand on the matter."[11]

Brezhnev responded on the occasion of International Solidarity Day with the Palestinian People, November 28, 1980. It was
then that he sent greetings to Arafat promising Moscow's "eter-
nal support" for the "just cause" of the Palestinians.[12]

Opportunities for high-level contacts continued in 1981. When
the 26th Party Congress met in Moscow in February, Farouk
Kaddoumi and a PLO delegation participated. Addressing the
PLO directly at the opening session on the 23d, Brezhnev said:
"The USSR continues to be convinced that the Israeli occupa-
tion of all the Arab territories captured in 1967 must be halted.
The inalienable rights of the Palestinian Arab people must be
realized, including the right to establish their own state."[13]

When Brezhnev informed Arafat in October 1981 that the
PLO Mission in Moscow had been granted official diplomatic
status, he reiterated his message of support[14] and wished the
Palestinian people further successes in their struggle for a just
peace in the Mideast, for achieving national independence, and
for establishing their own state. "The Soviet Union," he said,
"loyal to the Leninist principles of solidarity with the peoples

fighting for their national liberation, will always side with the Palestinians' just cause."[15]

When *TASS* reported the October meeting of Brezhnev and Arafat, it said, they "resolutely rejected the attempts made by the participants in the Camp David deal to substitute talk about so-called 'autonomy for the Palestinians' for the solution of the fundamental issue, namely, granting the Arab people of Palestine the right to exercise their legitimate right of self-determination and national statehood."[16]

These high-level contacts in Moscow produced significant political results. In addition, Arafat and his representatives frequently met with Soviet officials at other locations, including Algiers, Damascus, Tunis, and New York City at the United Nations. Regular contacts have also been maintained with Bulgaria, Czechoslovakia, East Germany, Hungary, Poland, and Yugoslavia, where the PLO established offices.

Even after the defeat of the PLO in Lebanon in the summer of 1982, Brezhnev declared that the Palestinian cause "will eventually triumph." In a message to Arafat he confirmed "that the Soviet Union was and remains on the side of the Arab people of Palestine and their only legitimate representative, the PLO."[17]

Just three months after Brezhnev's death, Andropov maintained that Moscow would support the Palestinian people until they recover their legitimate rights.[18] More recently, against the backdrop of mutiny within the PLO ranks, the Soviet leader sent a message in which he emphasized the importance of a "strong and unified position, based on the relationship between the PLO and Syria, as well as Palestinian unity under its legitimate leadership, headed by Chairman Arafat."

Similar expressions of support have been given by East European countries. Suffice it to mention the assertion made by the Bulgarian delegate at the Palestine National Council in Algiers in February 1983 "that the Palestinian fighters who stood fast in Beirut proved that no force in the world can liquidate the Palestinian revolution."[19]

It is therefore not surprising that the Soviet media have consistently regarded PLO terrorist attacks as "legitimate wars of liberation." For example, the assault on March 18, 1978, on the coastal road in Israel during which forty civilians died and sixty were wounded, was described by *Radio Moscow* in Arabic as a "military operation." The broadcast further declared that the Palestinians, led by the PLO, have the right to utilize all forms of military-political combat in order to achieve their goals against the "Imperialists and the Zionists" and to succeed in "their return to the homeland." Moreover, *TASS* called the attack "an Israeli provocation," carried out as a pretext to invade Lebanon and compared Israeli actions to the Nazi operations in the conquest of Poland.

The repeated theme of Soviet political affinity with the PLO is seen, for instance, in the *Izvestia* statement of November 26, 1980: "The USSR has always supported, and continues to support, the struggle of the Palestinian people for their legitimate inalienable national rights, including the establishment of a sovereign Palestinian state. It supports the elimination of all the results of Israeli aggression since 1967." On the following day *Pravda* asserted: "The USSR has supported and is consistently and firmly supporting the Palestinian people. Amicable Soviet-Palestinian relations are gradually developing and strengthening. The USSR is a faithful ally of the Palestinian people and of other Arab peoples in their struggle to ensure their national rights and to achieve peace and stability in the Middle East."

Clearly, the Soviet media have seized on every opportunity to attack Israel and the United States and thereby serve the political interest of the PLO. The recent events in Lebanon further illustrate this fact. On July 5, 1982, *Pravda* reported that U.S. military supplies—said to include napalm, cluster, and ball-bearing bombs—along with political support, especially the U.S. veto of the U.N. resolution for the withdrawal of Israeli troops, have aided Israeli "genocide" in Lebanon. According to the official press, the Zionists are driving the Lebanese people out of buildings and into concentration camps.

In September the news stories about Lebanon mounted and the accusations against Israel and U.S. assistance to Israel multiplied. When President-elect Bashir Gemayel was assassinated, an anonymous Soviet official, quoted in the Kuwaiti media, blamed the assassination on the Israeli intelligence service.[20] Similarly, in the aftermath of the massacre of Palestinian civilians at the Beirut refugee camps, Sabra and Shatila, the Soviet media excoriated Israel without restraint. Referring to the carnage in Beirut, *TASS* said the responsibility "rests also with those who armed the aggressor and, in fact, instigated the actions. If not for Washington's support, Israel would not have dared to commit such atrocities."[21] Two days later *TASS* reported that, according to PLO officials, "Washington knew in advance about the atrocious crime. . . . Nevertheless, the administration did absolutely nothing."[22]

In return for the foregoing political and diplomatic support, the PLO has played an active role in promoting Moscow's aims in the Mideast and beyond. Arafat set the tone for this policy with his appeal to the Palestinians and the Arabs, in general, "to adopt the most violent means against the United States and its interests in the region."[23]

Arafat has been consistently critical of Washington's position. For example, in an interview with *Literaturnaya Gazetta,* he said, "The United States is directly influencing the policy and actions of Begin. Washington influences Tel Aviv and not vice versa! Everything from the planning of Israeli policy to implementing it is controlled by the United States. . . . All the ambitions of the United States in the Middle East, coincide with the ambitions of Israel in that region."[24] In a speech to a visiting Soviet delegation in Beirut, Arafat "stressed that our relations with the Soviet Union are strategic and reflect that we are in the same trench, in the same position against imperialism, Zionism, racial colonialism, and fascism." He continued, "We look to you, comrade, the Central Committee of the Soviet Communist Party and the socialist bloc, full of hope, as friend to friend, [for] a view which the Soviet Union adopts in considering the questions of liberation and progress in the world."[25]

At a rally in Beirut in 1980, marking the fifty-sixth anniversary of the founding of the Lebanese Communist Party, Abu Iyad, Arafat's deputy, expressed a variation of the same theme by saying:

We, the members of the Communist Party and of the National Movement, are fighting together in the same foxhole, in order to arrive at a democratic state. . . . Our unity, together with the National Movement, extends its hand to the "Steadfastness Front" and to Syria, and congratulates our Syrian and Soviet brothers on the conclusion of their Friendship Pact, which we see as a step forward on the path to liberation. We believe that this pact includes us as well.[26]

A year later the PLO-Soviet common strategic aims, Abu Iyad said, were four:

1. To establish a sovereign Palestinian state under PLO control
2. To strengthen the Soviet-PLO alliance
3. To induce all Arab nations to "lift their embargo" on diplomatic relations with Moscow
4. To work for revolution in the Middle East—based on PLO Marxism and its "pan-Arab position"[27]

Representatives of various distinct groups that form the PLO have underscored and elaborated on these common interests. George Habash spoke on behalf of his organization, the Popular Front (PFLP), about unyielding antagonism for the United States:

We emphasize a firm and clear stand against imperialism and its interests in the region and affirm that imperialism—primarily American imperialism—is our principal enemy. Therefore the interests of the United States in the area should be crushed, and any thought that that country could be neutral in our conflict with the Zionist enemy should be abolished and rejected.[28]

Thus, Khaled al-Fahum, Chairman of the Palestine National Council, suggested the following course of action:

It might begin by imposing a popular general economic boycott on American interests and economy. This will create pressure on most of the Arab governments, so that they will impose the economic boycott on their behalf—whether by the use of oil, or by withdrawing their deposits in the financial institutions and boycotting American goods. This requires cooperation on the popular level in all the Arab states, so that this popular pressure becomes an influential factor on most Arab governments.[29]

Similarly, Fatah's Fourth General Conference held in Damascus in May 1980 called for "the strengthening of the strategic alliance with the socialist states and, foremostly, with the USSR, since this alliance is necessary for effectively containing the American and Zionist policy against the Palestinian cause and that of liberation throughout the world."

Farouk Kaddoumi, focusing on Moscow's concerns in the Persian Gulf states, said:

> We are interested in the development of good relations between our friends, the Soviet Union, and the Kingdom of Saudi Arabia. Good relations between these two countries would prove beyond doubt that the imaginary Soviet threat which the United States is trying to create in the region does not exist. . . . It is necessary for Saudi Arabia, the greatest economic power in the Arab world, to be on good terms with the Soviet Union.[30]

Warning of adverse consequences if the United States moves into the Persian Gulf or into Saudi Arabia to protect the flow of oil, Arafat promised, "We shall set petroleum ablaze if the American forces try to approach it. We shall set it alight in defense of Arab petroleum."[31]

Moreover, recent Soviet political maneuvering in the Persian Gulf region has been supported by PLO activities. Abu Mazin, a member of the PLO Executive Committee, tried to promote Moscow's commercial plans in the United Arab Emirates. His efforts included accompanying a Soviet press delegation during a visit to Abu Dhabi in May 1983.[32]

The PLO's ideological and political identification with Moscow's strategic interests beyond the region is also evident. On one occasion the PLO representative at the Islamic Foreign Ministers' Conference in Dakar in July 1978 went to great lengths to defend the Soviet Union against the charge that it had intervened in Africa's internal affairs.[33] In the following year, reports emerged that the PLO had coordinated its activities in Iran with Moscow.[34] Thus, Abu Iyad declared:

> The Palestinian revolution, which is following the dangerous military moves of the United States and several of its allies in the area,

cannot sit with its arms folded and view these actions as directed against it, since it is affiliated strategically with the Iranian revolution. Therefore, the Palestinian revolution announces that it will stand steadfastly at the side of the Iranian people against the plots of American imperialism.[35]

The PLO also expressed its strong support of the Soviet invasion of Afghanistan. According to Yassir Abd Rabhi, who directed the PLO's Department of Information and Culture, "The Russian involvement in Afghanistan is an important asset to all revolutionary forces which oppose the expansion of the American presence in the Middle East."[36] Bassam Abu Sherif, speaking for the Popular Front (PFLP) added, "The Russians have helped progressive forces in Afghanistan to foil efforts by pro-U.S. elements to take control of the nation's institutions. The Americans have backed opponents of the Afghan government in an attempt to counter blows to the United States in neighbouring Iran. . . . Western hypocrisy was underlined by the fact that the United States and its Western friends were bitterly opposed to the Islamic forces in Afghanistan."[37]

As for the PLO's stand toward the NATO alliance, Issam Sartawi, the late PLO representative in Europe, asserted:

A central tactic in the PLO's propaganda campaign in Western Europe is to accentuate the political, economic, and strategic differences between the United States and its European allies. That is, the greater the split between Western Europe and the United States, the more enhanced is the PLO's ability to maneuver, the better its image in the eyes of Western European leaders, and the stronger the organization then appears in the eyes of the United States, thus allowing the USSR to benefit from the undermining of the Western Bloc.[38]

Summing up the rationale for the Soviet-PLO linkage, Abu Iyad stated: "If we had the capacity to sign [a] treaty with the Soviet Union, we would have signed a thousand treaties, and if we controlled land, we would have allowed the Soviets a thousand bases, because we are dealing with a foe stronger than Israel, the United States."[39]

In short, the PLO and the Soviet Union share interests that focus on the need to combat "American imperialism and Zionism." Despite potential differences of opinion with the PLO on issues concerning a final settlement of the Palestinian question, the Soviet Union is not ready for a rift with the PLO and most likely will always stand by it publicly. In its attempts to influence the PLO, the Soviets raise tactical considerations, primarily in terms of the need for flexibility and political realism. The Soviet Union is asking the PLO to strive to achieve what can be achieved rather than attempt to realize all its declared aspirations. This safer course is what Arafat had espoused and what is now under attack by Syrian and Libyan supported militants in the PLO.

As a result of their mutual interests, the Soviet Union and the PLO have opened extensive cultural and scientific contacts. Three in 1980 alone show the range and diversity of agreements signed. In March the Association of Palestinian Jurists and the Union of Soviet Jurists agreed on mutual cooperation and exchange; in November the General Secretariat of the Association of Palestinian Authors and Journalists met with the Union of Soviet Newspapermen;[40] and in December the Palestinian News Agency *(WAFA)* and the Soviet Press Agency *(Novosti)* issued a statement entitled "Information and the Call of Peace and Friendship Between the Two Peoples." This document includes sections dealing with cooperation and coordination in the area of information, as well as an agreement to commemorate the anniversaries of the deaths of two Palestinian writers in simultaneous ceremonies in Moscow and Beirut, arranged by the Soviet Middle East Studies Institute and the Palestinian-Soviet Friendship Association.[41] Finally, the Palestinian-Soviet Friendship Association inaugurated its house in Beirut in the presence of Arafat and Ambassador Aleksandr Soldatov on March 8, 1981.

It should also be mentioned that the PLO developed similar treaties of cooperation with Soviet allies—with East Germany in September 1980 and with Czechoslovakia and Bulgaria in January 1981.[42]

Operational Linkages

Committed to strengthening Palestinian militancy, especially through terrorist activities in the Mideast and beyond, the Soviet

Union began channeling funds and other assistance directly and through intermediaries as early as 1969.[43] After that, the ties steadily grew. Evidence of close military relationships, particularly intelligence linkages, training, and supply of weapons, is ample.

Several examples illustrate Soviet-PLO cooperation in the intelligence area. In 1979 a wide-ranging Soviet intelligence network was reported to exist in Pakistan, aided by Palestinian terrorists. The Soviet Ambassador to Pakistan, Sarvar A. Azimov, who was formerly stationed in Beirut, was reportedly in charge of the operation, and he used the PLO ties he had made during his stay in Lebanon. One of his associates was Zaiden Uni Mahmoud, a Palestinian pilot cadet. When arrested by the Pakistani authorities, the Palestinian was found to be carrying secret documents to be forwarded to the Russians.[44]

On March 15, 1980, Arafat reported to Ambassador Soldatov in Beirut on a trip to the Persian Gulf area taken by Abu Iyad, then chief of PLO intelligence and internal security. The purpose of Iyad's trip was to meet with Abu Jihad, in charge of PLO cells in the area, and to explore prospects for expanding covert PLO activity among the Palestinian communities in Saudi Arabia, Kuwait, and the United Arab Emirates. On March 17, Abu Jihad left on a secret visit to Moscow. Western sources believe his trip was connected with the PLO plan to set up efforts to destabilize "conservative" Gulf regimes.[45]

During the same year, evidence of Soviet involvement in the transfer of intelligence information to the PLO came to light when a citizen of Greece was captured by Israeli security forces and charged with espionage. The Greek, a newspaper photographer, admitted that he had routinely sent to Nicosia photographs of Israeli sites that were vulnerable to terrorist attack and that these photographs had been forwarded from Nicosia to East Berlin and then handed over to the KGB. The KGB transferred them to the PLO and other international terrorists to whom they were of interest.[46]

In early 1981, Dr. Johar Sayag, an Arab physician from Bir Zeit, near Ramallah on the West Bank, was discovered to have been recruited by the KGB while a student in Moscow. Sayag had been sent back to the West Bank to gather information, which he relayed to the Russians via Jordan's capital city, Amman. The information was shared with the PLO.[47]

Among documents captured by the Israeli forces in Lebanon in the summer of 1982, a letter written by a staff member of the Iranian Embassy in Beirut to his superiors at the Iranian Foreign Ministry tells of a KGB spy working in the embassy with the cooperation of Fatah. The staff member charges that the spy, one Ahmed Mawahdi, incited embassy workers and caused problems among the Shi'ites in Lebanon, who had been friendly to Iran's Islamic Revolution. Another document, dated August 23, 1981, and signed by a PLO security officer, reports that the Russian military attaché in Beirut informed the PLO about Israeli efforts to acquire British military equipment during visits by an Israeli Navy officer in Singapore and Malta.

Finally, it is noteworthy that the operational and intelligence-gathering activities for the PLO are carefully delegated by Moscow to East European countries. They supply intelligence information to the PLO and serve as a launching area for various terrorist operations. For example, in East Germany the espionage service supplied PLO terrorists with important information for carrying out an attack against industrial installations in West Berlin. A group of PLO terrorists, arrested by West German police, admitted this fact. Also Czechoslovakia is known to have been the home training base of the terrorists who took over a train in Austria on September 28, 1973. The train was carrying emigrants from the Soviet Union.[48]

A major element of Soviet-PLO cooperation is in the field of training. The evidence of an intimate relationship is overwhelming. Various intelligence sources have reported on the existence of an elaborate infrastructure of over forty training camps within the Soviet Union. The camps in Moscow, Tashkent, Batum on the Black Sea, Odessa, Baku, and Simferopol, the major base known for the Soviet Academy for Military Training, give special attention to intelligence. The Third Department of the GRU (Soviet Military Intelligence) in close cooperation with the KGB, provides direct military instruction for terrorists. It is estimated that the Soviet Union spends more than U.S. $200 million per year on training within the country. The KGB also operates training camps in Eastern Europe. The most active are those in East Germany in the vicinity of Pankow and Finsterwalde; in Bulgaria at Varna; in Czechoslovakia at Karlovy Vary and Ostrava; and in Hungary near Lake Balaton.[49]

Thousands of PLO members have been trained by Soviet and satellite instructors at these and other installations in staff and command courses, as well as a variety of professional subjects such as communications, electronics, engineering, artillery, pilot training, biological and chemical warfare, and military weapons maintenance. They also learn specific techniques such as the preparation of electrical charges, the production of incendiary devices, and the methods of exploding metals and destructing bridges. In 1981 East Germany, under agreement with Arafat, offered to assign fifty military advisers to help train PLO members.[50]

In September 1979, Zehdi Labib Terzi, the PLO's observer at the United Nations, openly admitted these strong ties. He stated publicly that "the Soviet Union and all the socialist countries . . . open their military academies to some of our freedom fighters."[51] He later gave further details indicating that hundreds of Palestinian fighters at the level of brigade commander have graduated from Soviet military academies, and that some two thousand Palestinian students were currently studying at Soviet schools, mostly in scientific and technical fields. He added that three hundred scholarships a year are reserved for the PLO.[52] The head of the Palestine Liberation Army, Tala'at Yakoub, confirmed the Soviet training links by saying simply, "Every year we send some of our personnel to train in the Soviet Union."[53]

A Fatah officer aboard the Greek ship *Agios Demetrios,* detained by Israel in the Gulf of Eilat on September 9, 1978, admitted that he was trained "in military engineering at a camp in the Black Sea area." He said he had undergone a six-month course, which included—in addition to engineering—political instruction on the Russian Revolution, Communism, and Socialism. He noted that the course, given without charge, was designated for members of "liberation movements" from all over the world. He said he himself had been trained to serve as an instructor for Fatah in Lebanon.[54]

Adnan Jaber, the captured commander of the cell that carried out an attack in Hebron on May 2, 1980, confessed that he had undergone six months of military training in the Soviet Union in 1974 with a group of seventy Palestinians—members of Fatah, the Popular Frent (PFLP), the Democratic Front (DFLP), Sa'iqa, the Arab Liberation Front, and the Popular Struggle Front. The group was based at a country estate near the town of Skhodnya, twenty miles outside Moscow. The training included political instruction, tactical military exercises, the use of light arms and hand grenades, the production and concealment of explosive matériel, topography, and communication. He revealed that PLO personnel also receive training in China, Vietnam, and North Korea; that the various PLO factions train together in the Soviet Union and on PLO bases in Lebanon and Syria; and that political differences do not interfere with the training.[55]

Although the Israeli forces discovered a number of Soviet documents, including maps and certificates illustrating the nature of PLO training, during "Operation Litani" in March 1978, it was not until "Operation Peace for Galilee" in the summer of 1982 that numerous captured documents illuminated Moscow's training efforts dramatically.[56] These documents show that Soviet and East European military and civilian training for the PLO dates back at least to 1973. The scale and variety of recent activity in this area, combined with the volume of arms shipments, indicate that the Soviet Union aimed at building the terrorist militia into a sizable regular army. The evidence includes numerous graduation certificates of PLO personnel, master lists of those who had completed military studies, and instructions for those wishing to participate.

A document dated February 22, 1982, revealed the names of PLO personnel who had taken courses in the Soviet Union that prepared them for the following positions: battalion commander, battalion staff officer, deputy battalion commander for political subjects, infantry instructor, anti-aircraft battery commander, military engineering platoon commander, improved Strela-2 operator, and commander of 82mm mortar batteries. Another document, dated October 22, 1981, listed various air defense courses that had been held in the Soviet Union in September and December 1977 and in November 1978. Files contained snapshots of PLO men and others undergoing training.

Among the graduation certificates, uncovered in "Operation Peace for Galilee," was one issued by the Soviet Ministry of Defense to PLO Captain Abdul Aziz Mahmud Abu Fadah, who was trained at the Vistral Academy in the Soviet Union from October 1978 to March 1979. His certificate, with the rank of infantry regiment commander, was signed by the academy commander, General Folkovnik D. Dargonsky. A certificate addressed to Lieutenant Colonel Bashad Ahmed Abdul Aziz an-Nabris is proof that he completed a course for tank battalion commanders held from September 1980 to January 1981. Other documents in the collection recorded Soviet courses in infantry, engineering, armor, and artillery branches of an army, as well as Marxist-Leninist political indoctrination.

Documents found in Fatah headquarters in Sidon, Lebanon, register some of the courses offered in Eastern Europe along with the names of PLO participants, most of them from Fatah itself. The men were enrolled in artillery, armor, and engineering courses at the military college in East Germany; in armor and air defense courses at the Hungarian military college; in courses for brigade staff officers, battalion commanders, battery commanders, and noncommissioned officers in Bulgaria; and in command and staff courses in Yugoslavia. Even in these eastern European countries, Russian equipment was generally used. Documents refer to 37mm anti-aircraft cannon, mortars, and standard and improved SAM-7 missiles.

As early as 1974, training courses were offered to the best and most promising members of several different PLO groups. When those selected completed their training, they became available as cadremen and instructors who passed on their knowledge to recruits at PLO camps in the Arab world and beyond.

What all these captured documents add up to is that the Soviet Union undertook to provide training for some three to four thousand terrorists for Fatah in the Soviet Union and Eastern

Europe. With East German instructors predominating, the main training centers in 1978 were in East Germany, Czechoslovakia, and Hungary, as well as in South Yemen and Iraq. Fatah received two-thirds of the training openings in the Soviet Union, and various other factions of the PLO divided the remainder. At least one thousand Arab Palestinians have already been trained in Soviet bloc camps.

The news media have continuously followed and detailed many of these developments, but inevitably in sketchy and piecemeal fashion often unnoted in the United States. For instance, one news report indicated that Simferopol was a primary reception center for PLO members chosen for sabotage and terrorist training in the Soviet Union. Simferopol, the report stated, was also the setting for special courses in river crossing and all types of sabotage for 50 to 60 trainees.[57] Another report stated that 32 Palestinian pilots and 60 technicians completed training courses in the Soviet Union, East Germany, and Czechoslovakia,[58] and 150 Palestinian pilots underwent training in "socialist countries."[59]

An undated document of the Democratic Front (DFLP) lists those "friendly countries"—East Germany, Czechoslovakia, the Soviet Union, Bulgaria, and Romania—that provided scholarships for advanced study by members of the front in 1982. A Fatah document dated February 2, 1982, cites the prerequisites for study in the Soviet courses, which include a high school diploma and grades of over 60 percent. Candidates for advanced study were said to be selected by the Soviet-Palestinian Friendship Society. This system is not a casual or superficial effort.

The Soviet Arsenal of Liberation

An ever-increasing flow of arms and ammunition, manufactured in the Soviet Union, Czechoslovakia, and East Germany, have been shipped to the PLO via East Germany and Hungary. Nonetheless, the evidence proves conclusively that the Soviet Union itself has been the chief supplier of weapons to the PLO. George Habash has confirmed this relationship, reporting as early as 1970 on the availability of Soviet arms.[60] Since then other sources have elaborated on the Soviet-PLO arms linkage. The 1975 Senate Committee hearings on terrorist activities noted that the PLO received Soviet RPG-7 hand-held launchers and AK-47 and SKS carbines.[61] Specific information flows from media stories:

- On January 15, 1977, two vessels docking in Tyre unloaded Soviet arms and sophisticated missiles, some of them anti-aircraft missiles, for use by the PLO.[62]
- Soviet and Cuban embassies in Cyprus have a key role in smuggling arms to the PLO.[63]
- In January 1978 two vessels docked at Tyre delivered sophisticated missiles, among other things.[64]
- In August 1978 the PLO received sophisticated Soviet weaponry, including anti-tank and anti-aircraft systems.[65]
- Arms and terrorist matériel bearing markings of Soviet and Eastern European manufacture were found in Lebanon in March 1978.[66]
- Advanced Soviet arms were issued to the PLO in January 1979.[67]
- Two Soviet vessels docked in Tyre in August 1979 with a consignment of rockets, anti-tank shells, small arms, mortar bombs, and 160mm, 130mm, and 82mm cannons for the PLO.[68]
- The Fatah-controlled Palestine Liberation Army's Ein Jalyout Brigade received a consignment of twenty to twenty-five Soviet-made T-34 tanks, transferred to the PLO from Hungary via Syria in early 1980. The PLO received fifty T-34 tanks in May of that year.[69]
- The decision to supply the PLO with modern T-62 tanks was made at a meeting between Soviet Foreign Minister Andrei Gromyko and Yasser Arafat in January 1980.[70]
- Soviet arms were to have been unloaded in Tyre in December 1980. They included seventeen tanks, rocket launchers, and ammunition.[71]
- The PLO and Yugoslavia concluded a number of military agreements, including one that Yugoslavia would supply heavy artillery, surface-to-air missiles, and other arms to the PLO.[72]

- During August 1981, in Moscow, a Palestinian delegation signed a weaponry supply agreement that included SAM-6 and submarine missiles.[73]
- In October 1981 Soviet arms were supplied to the PLO through Libya.[74]
- In November 1981 Soviet arms were supplied to the PLO through Libya.[75]
- During the same month military agreements were signed by Abu Iyad with the Soviet Union and East Germany.[76]
- In November 1981 Abu Jihad discussed military cooperation in East Germany and Hungary.[77] He later confirmed the cooperative arrangements with these countries.[78]
- In December 1981 Soviet weaponry and ammunition were supplied by Cuba to the Popular Front (PFLP).[79]

Probably one of the most active periods of Soviet-PLO arms cooperation occurred between July 1981 and June 1982 when the cease-fire along the Lebanese-Israeli border negotiated by Philip Habib was in force. The PLO, during that time, reinforced its supplies with massive quantities of weapons and ammunition—mostly Soviet-made. These supplies arrived in Lebanon by air, sea, and land. According to Israeli intelligence estimates:[80]

- Twenty T-54 and T-55 tanks were added to the 60 T-34 tanks already in use.
- Forty 130mm long-range cannons were added to the 50 in place before the cease-fire; 48 were deployed in the south, as compared with 23 before July 1981.
- The number of BM-21 rocket launchers (Katyushas, equipped with 40 barrels apiece) was doubled from 40 to 80.
- Anti-tank cannons were more than doubled, from 60 to 150; of these, 77 were deployed in South Lebanon.
- The number of 120mm and 160mm mortars was doubled to about 200.
- The PLO acquired four-barreled ZSU-4 radar-guided anti-aircraft cannons mounted on armored personnel carriers to supplement its 14.5mm anti-aircraft cannon and SAM-7 shoulder-launched missiles.

- A 500-man Libyan SAM-9 anti-aircraft missile unit arrived in Lebanon to aid the PLO.
- Libya also supplied the PLO with two 37-meter gunboats, anchored in Syrian ports.

In Lebanon, during and after the hostilities in the summer of 1982, the Israeli forces were surprised to discover that the actual amount of arms they had seized far exceeded any of their previous estimates. The combat matériel uncovered by October 1982 in some 540 southern Lebanese and West Beirut weapons depots was enough to equip several infantry brigades and artillery units. When the Israelis transported this cache to their homeland, they filled 4,300 trucks. The supplies were:

- 5,630 tons of ammunition
- 1,320 armed combat and other vehicles including several hundred tanks of the T-34, T-55, and T-62 varieties
- 33,303 small arms
- 1,352 anti-tank weapons, including 1,099 personal weapons; 27 anti-tank missile launchers; 138 recoilless rifles; and 88 anti-tank guns
- 215 mortars (60mm, 81mm, 82mm, 120mm, and 160mm)
- 62 Katyusha rocket launchers
- 82 field artillery pieces (122mm, 130mm, 155mm, and 25-pound guns)
- 196 anti-aircraft weapons, including 43 AA machine guns; 153 AA guns (20mm, 23mm, 30mm, 37mm, 40mm, 57mm, and 100mm)
- 2,204 communications instruments
- 2,387 optical instruments (e.g., telescopes, binoculars, and periscopes)[81]

A wide variety of arms and ammunition came from the Soviet Union and East European countries, with substantial contributions from China, North Korea, and Vietnam. Some also originated in the West, but it is primarily the Soviet-sponsored arms buildup that has increased the PLO's military potential vis-à-vis Israel and the Lebanese governments. Moreover, since the number and types of weapons are not commonly associated with traditional terrorist activities, it can be assumed that the stock-pile could have been used ultimately by Syria or even the Soviet Union in any major regional conflict that developed out of PLO destabilizing actions. Perhaps this is the reason Moscow continues to bolster the PLO arsenal. Recent reports indicate that Palestinian forces in the Al-Ba'aqa Valley in the eastern Lebanese region have received fifteen Soviet-made T-54 tanks. They are being operated by PLO members who were trained in Syrian PLO camps.[82] And finally, a three-year Soviet-PLO military supply agreement was signed in June 1983.[83]

Moreover, various documents, found in Lebanon illuminate the nature and extent of the PLO-East European ties. A case in point is a May 1982 document that contains the minutes of talks held the preceding month between East German and Hungarian officials and the PLO military delegation. The talks concerned arms and ammunition agreements and training for PLO officers in the military academies of the two nations. In the course of deliberations, the East German defense minister asked for a list of required equipment so he could submit it for approval "in the name of the Party and the State."

The PLO itemized MB-41 machine guns and ammunition, 57mm anti-aircraft cannons and ammunition, and such auxiliary equipment as field glasses, medicine, and blankets, The minutes of April 17, 1982, added Shilka NK 1s; 37mm, 57mm, 100mm, and 122mm cannons and ammunition; automatic and improved automatic rifles; engineering and artillery equipment, and more.

On April 25, 1982, the PLO delegation met with Hungarian Defense Ministry personnel and visited the commercial weapons firm Technikal. The company's deputy director-general gave a report on various items ordered by the PLO that were currently being stored at company facilities or at military warehouses. These items comprised spare parts for T-34 tanks, 122mm shrapnel shells, and mortar shells and ammunition.

This is the case history, with the facts that are now known, of Soviet support for the PLO's military prowess. In 1982 the estimated PLO armed guerrilla force actively engaged in the Mideast numbered more than 22,000 with 7,100 in West Beirut and 15,000 in other parts of Lebanon and in Syria. In this most productive proving ground, the PLO flourished. Countless more, under various auspices controlled by Arafat's Fatah or closely associated with it, operated elsewhere. This guerrilla force is drawn from a total of approximately 4 million Palestinians, living not only in the Mideast but elsewhere in the world.

When member states of the Warsaw Treaty met in Prague on January 5, 1983, Andropov signed the communiqué that called on the PLO, as the only legitimate representative of the Arab people of Palestine, to join in drafting and adopting international guarantees for peaceful settlements of conflicts, not only in the Mideast, but worldwide. The PLO reaching out in all directions with armies and assassin squads against "imperialist" forces, whom the Soviet Union accuses of disregard for the "basic rights" and "vital interests" of peoples seeking national liberation.[84]

Chapter 5

International Infrastructure of Terrorism

Despite the circumstantial nature of much of the evidence, it is obvious from the PLO documents that there exists a carefully developed international terrorist infrastructure that serves Moscow's foreign policy objectives of destabilizing non-Communist governments. In recent years, Syria as a base and Lebanon as a target provide the most conspicuous examples, but they are rivaled now by Nicaragua as a base and El Salvador as a target. The PLO outreach is obvious in many areas, and the infrastructure is in place in each of the major trouble spots in the world.

The Moscow Nerve Center

The International Department of the Central Committee of the Communist Party of the Soviet Union, the Soviet Security Agency (KGB), and the Soviet Military Intelligence (GRU) have played the major role in building and guiding this operational network. Of these three, the Party's International Department, headed by Boris Ponomarev, has been the most important Soviet agency for the support of terrorism. It has consistently promoted widespread revolutionary violence even while taking care to project the illusory image that the Soviet Union was abiding by the spirit of peaceful coexistence. Setting the tone for the real mission of the agency, Ponomarev declared in 1964:

> We understand our international duty as consisting in support for all the revolutionary, democratic movements of modern times. . . . We Soviet Communists call upon all the fraternal parties and all the revolutionary forces to close their ranks more tightly, to overcome all difficulties, to rally under the banner of Marxism-Leninism in the name of the triumph of the working class.[1]

To facilitate the Communist Party's activities, Stalin established the Lenin Institute (also known as the Institute of Social Studies, the Institute of Social Sciences, or the International School of Marxism-Leninism). Located in Moscow, the institute is directed by F. D. Ryzhenko, who has G. P. Chernikov and V. G. Pribytov as his deputies responsible for supervision of the curriculum and liaison with the Party's Central Committee. Select members of Western and Third World Communist political organizations following the Soviet line have been trained there in propaganda and psychological warfare, armed and unarmed combat, and guerrilla warfare—the core curriculum in international terrorism.

In 1958, Khrushchev founded Moscow's Patrice Lumumba Friendship University to serve as a base for the indoctrination and training of potential freedom fighters from the Third World who are not Communist Party members.[2] More specialized training in terrorism is provided in Baku, Odessa, Simferopol, Tashkent, and in the suburbs of Moscow. At these locations the techniques of guerrilla warfare and other skills—including the use of explosives, mining of transportation routes, commando field tactics, and the combat capabilities of shoulder-fired rockets—are being taught to many revolutionaries, including first and foremost the PLO.

In addition, the Communist Party has sometimes set up terrorist groups for its own purposes quite far afield from its main operational areas of concentration. There is evidence, for example, that it played a role in the establishment of the Solidarité and Aide et Amitié terrorist network in Paris. Directed by Henri Curiel, a Communist Egyptian Jew who died in 1978, this network had connections with some seventeen illegal groups, among them being the Popular Revolutionary Vanguard (VPR) in Brazil, the Movement of the Revolutionary Left (MLR) in Uruguay and Chile, the Quebec Liberation Front (FLQ), and the African National Congress (ANC) in South Africa.[3]

The KGB, which Andropov headed for fifteen years before he became chief of the Soviet Communist Party and state, has established courses for training terrorists not only in the Soviet Union but also in East Germany. The instruction covers all aspects of terrorist activities, such as surveillance methods—how to follow without being detected and how to escape when being tailed—how to use disguises, how to create and use fake identities, how to use modern weaponry, including SAM-7 hand-held missiles and anti-tank guns, and even how to organize and run a terrorist network. During Yuri Andropov's chairmanship, the KGB operated a special section for recruiting and training of terrorists at its Moscow headquarters.[4]

The KGB and the GRU have tried to establish a number of terrorist movements or to gain control of existing ones. A defecting KGB officer, V. N. Sakharov, has revealed that the KGB sought to form terrorist cells in Saudi Arabia, Turkey, and in the smaller Arab states in the Persian Gulf. There were similar clandestine Soviet efforts in the early 1970s to penetrate and control the Palestinian movement from within, a campaign that paid off in Syria and Lebanon. Attempts have been made by KGB members to establish links with the Irish Republican Army itself.

Many of these groups are interconnected. Robert Sikes, a Democrat from Florida serving in the U.S. Congress, charged that Iranian terrorists were closely linked with the Red Brigades in Italy, the Baader-Meinhof Gang in West Germany, and the Popular Front (PFLP). He further charged that "key members were schooled in the Soviet Union."[5]

Moscow's involvement is for the most part clandestine. Commenting on this aspect a Turkish scholar, Aydin Yalcin, observed:

> General Evren pointed out in a February 1981 press conference that the total amount of money obtained by Turkish terrorists from extortions and bank robberies constitutes only 2 percent of the hundreds of millions of dollars of weapons and ammunition available to terrorists. Although General Evren was reluctant to name the Soviet Union directly, he asked, "Where does it come from if not from a rich external power?"[6]

Other scholars, among them Brian Crozier of the Institute of the Study of Conflict in London, have named the Soviet Union as giving direct support to terrorists.

Although the Baader-Meinhof Gang is openly critical of the Soviet Union, it was secretly subsidized by the East Germans, whose Ministry of State Security is under the control of the KGB. This gang evolved out of the collaborators of a journal of the extreme left entitled *Konkret,* edited by Klaus Rainer Rohl, whose wife was Ulrike Meinhof. Both were secret members of the Communist Party from 1956 to 1964, and Rohl received about $250,000 (some sources say $400,000) in subsidies through East Berlin and Prague.[7]

Many case histories have confirmed and added details about the Soviet role:

- Four Syrian terrorists arrested in 1975 by Dutch police admitted, under questioning, that they had been trained in weaponry, explosives, and propaganda at a small town near Moscow.[8]
- The Soviet Union carries on a program of recruiting young revolutionaries from all parts of the Third World to the Soviet Union for training and indoctrination.[9]
- Illich Ramirez Sanchez ("Carlos"), who participated in several terrorist attacks, was trained in Cuba, in the Patrice Lumumba Friendship University, and in Popular Front (PFLP) camps. At the university, his course work included training in assassination, sabotage, surveillance, weaponry use, and unarmed combat. His instructors were Soviet KGB agents.[10] It was Carlos who established liaisons between the late Dr. Wadi Haddad, Chief of Operations for the Popular Front (PFLP), the West German Red Army Faction (RAF), the Japanese United Red Army (URA), the Turkish Peoples' Liberation Army (TPLA), and the Italian Red Brigades, thus earning him the support of all these groups and the title of "International Jackal."
- Turkish left-wing groups, including the Turkish Peoples' Liberation Army, are aided and financed by the Soviet Union.[11]
- Baader-Meinhof Gang members constantly received support from the East German secret police. False papers and identity cards, money, arms, ammunition, and terrorist training were the specific forms of support.[12]
- According to the Italian publication *Il Settimanale* "countries

such as East Germany have a front-line position, along with Czechoslovakia and Libya, where they have training camps frequented by Argentines, Italians, Palestinians, Frenchmen, Germans, and members of the Irish Republican Army."

- KGB specialists established camps in Bulgaria (Varna), Czechoslovakia (Karlovy Vary and Dupov), East Germany (Finsterwalde), and Hungary (Lake Vara).

- Militants who were holding some fifty American hostages at the U.S. Embassy in Tehran included graduates of Soviet training centers in East Germany and Czechoslovakia.

- *Die Welt*, a leading conservative daily, quoted "Western diplomats" as saying members of the "hard-core" faction, which led the takeover of the U.S. Embassy on November 4, 1969, had been trained by Soviet and East German agents in East Berlin, Leipzig, and Prague.

- President Abolhassan Bani-Sadr of Iran said in an interview published by the Paris newspaper *Le Monde* that some of the militants were under Communist influence. Bani-Sadr sought unsuccessfully to transfer control of the American hostages from the militants to his own government.

- A West German newspaper said the Soviets and their allies recruited the alleged agents from Iranian exile student groups in Europe and that some of them had taken part in demonstrations at Iranian government missions in Switzerland in 1976 and the Netherlands in 1978. The newspaper gave no figures on how many militants were part of the pro-Moscow group.

- Terrorists from Italy who are known to have visited and/or spent time in Czechoslovakia (some repeatedly) are Giangiacomo Feltrinelli, Renato Curcio, Alberto Franceschini, Fabrizio Pelli, and Augusto Viel. Reports have been circulating for some time that the Czechs have set up a center in Karlovy Vary for the training of agents in destabilization operations. Czech-made keys were found in one of several hideouts of the Red Brigades uncovered by the police.

- Member of Parliament Vito Miceli, who had previously served with the rank of general as the head of the Italian intelligence (SID), made a statement on May 14, 1978, of the connections between Italian terrorism and the East European patron states. He said that on May 9, 1972, SID reported to the Minister of Defense proof of existing links between Feltrinelli, subversive groups of Italy's extreme left, and KGB agents working under diplomatic cover in the Soviet Embassy in Rome. At that time, SID recommended the expulsion of twenty-two Soviet agents from Italy. Although both the Defense Minister (Restivi) and the Foreign Minister (Moro) were in agreement with the proposed measure, it was vetoed by the then Prime Minister (Andreotti).[13]

- The most dramatic example of solidarity in Europe is the Bulgarian-KGB link to the Turkish terrorist who attempted to assassinate the Pope in 1981. The evidence, though not conclusive as to Soviet intent, includes information from a Bulgarian official who defected in France in July 1981 and strongly confirms Soviet use of Bulgaria as an operational base against both Italy and Turkey.[14]

North Korean Links with the Soviet Infrastructure

- Beginning in 1967–1969, terrorist training centers were established in North Korea, whose Communist regime is dominated by the Soviet Union and dependent on Soviet military assistance. In that period Moscow was more intent on concealing its role than it is now, and the remoteness of Korea originally helped maintain secrecy. The trainees eventually, however, have been traced to and in some cases apprehended in Latin America (Mexico, Brazil, Bolivia, Colombia), the Mideast, and Asia (Sri Lanka, Malaya, and Indonesia).[15]
- Some 2,500 terrorists and guerrillas, according to evidence supplied to Congress, have been trained in North Korean camps.[16]
- Terrorists arrested by the Iranian government in 1972 admitted that they had been indoctrinated and trained in North Korea.[17]
- Safe conduct out of Singapore for Palestinians and Japanese who tried to blow up an oil refinery was arranged by the government of North Korea.[18]
- North Korean diplomats overseas help coordinate the ac-

tivities of terrorists in Europe through an agent in East Germany.[19]

- Members of the Japanese Red Army provided sanctuary by North Korea in 1970 after they hijacked a Japan Air Lines aircraft.[20]

Southern Africa Infrastructure

The terrorist linkages extend from Moscow not only to Korea but as far as the tip of the continent of Africa. On March 22, 1982, Senator Denton, in his opening statement before the Subcommittee on Security and Terrorism of the Senate's Committee on the Judiciary, gave details on the role of the Soviet Union, Cuba, and East Germany in fomenting terrorism from bases in Angola, Mozambique, and other states bordering Namibia and South Africa. He said, "The presidents of both SWAPO (Sam Nujoma) and the ANC (Nelson Mandela) have repeatedly acknowledged the importance of Soviet support to their organizations."[21]

High officials of the South-West African People's Organization (SWAPO) and the African National Congress (ANC) were among the speakers at the 26th Party Congress in Moscow at the closing sessions in March 1981. In his address to the Congress, SWAPO's Nujoma described Soviet President Brezhnev as a "devoted, staunch fighter for peace, détente, freedom, and the people's rights and human dignity of all the world's people." Nujoma then directly acknowledged Soviet assistance to SWAPO by saying, "Without the support of the Soviet Union, we would not have been able to achieve those results that we have achieved today. . . . We address ourselves to the Soviet Union, which is giving comprehensive support to the people of Namibia."

During the hearings of Senator Denton's subcommittee, the members uncovered a successful plot hatched at the United Nations by SWAPO's president to assassinate two political rivals in Namibia. The subcommittee referred the details of the plot, and the supporting documents, to the Justice Department and the Attorney General of New York for investigation.

On March 25, 1982, Bartholomew Hlapane, a former member of the African National Congress and of the South African Communist Party, courageously testified before the subcommittee about the clandestine role of the South African Communist Party in the ANC and in the formation of the ANC's terrorist wing, Umkonto We Sizwe, "The Spear of the Nation." Before giving that testimony, Hlapane met with other witnesses, all former members of the ANC and SWAPO, to discuss the possible consequences of their testimony. Knowing they were marked for assassination, Hlapane and the other witnesses decided to tell their own stories and to expose the role of the Soviet Union and other Communist countries in subverting and exploiting the ANC and SWAPO.

On December 15, 1982, Hlapane was murdered along with his wife, in his home in Soweto, South Africa, by assassins using an AK-47 assault rifle. It appears that his fifteen-year-old daughter, Brenda, wounded in the attack, will be permanently paralyzed. Based on the modus operandi, the choice of weapon, and the release of a public statement taking credit for the murder, the killers were ANC terrorists.[22]

The PLO Outreach

The intimate Soviet-PLO relationship is beneficial in building linkages with wars of national liberation in many other parts of the world. The PLO is useful in its capacity as a resource center for terrorist organizations seeking to subvert non-Communist regimes anywhere. In carrying on low-intensity warfare, these organizations serve basic Soviet geopolitical interests of creating instability and unrest in nations where the Communists have a chance to gain political power.

Training

The PLO has trained some 10,000 terrorists from all regions of the world in its camps in Lebanon, Syria, Algeria, Iraq, Libya, and South Yemen. From January 1980 through June 1981 alone, 2,250 foreign terrorists from 28 countries in Europe, Latin America, Asia, and Africa participated in courses of one to four months' duration. For example, members of the Popular Front of the Arabian Peninsula, who were responsible for the attack on Mecca's Great Mosque in November 1979, were trained with members of the Popular Front (PFLP) in South Yemen by East German and Cuban instructors.

According to press reports, four members of the West German Red Army Faction, six members of the Italian Red Brigades, four members of the Japanese Red Army, three members of the Basque Separatists, 130 Turkish Armenian extremists, and 170 Iranian terrorists received training at the Palestinian Houmirriya camp south of Damascus in 1979–1980.[23] It has also been reported that 28 members of the Argentinian Monteneros, 12 operatives of the Brazilian Vanguarda, and 32 Asians, mostly from the Philippines, underwent similar training in PLO camps in Lebanon and Syria. An extensive PLO training and aid mission was virtually integrated into the Nicaraguan army framework with PLO instructors teaching the operation of Soviet equipment.

Arms

The PLO has served as a conduit for Soviet arms transactions with terrorist movements throughout the world. It is now clear that the PLO, as much as or more than Cuba, has been the main conduit for the Salvadoran opposition guerrilla forces. One arms delivery in early 1979, disguised as medical supplies, was intercepted by Moroccan authorities and never arrived in Nicaragua. In 1980 Fatah transferred weapons, mostly light arms and mortars, to the terrorists and guerrillas in Salvador. Moreover, expanded arms supplies for the leftists operating from Nicaragua were discussed during a visit by a PLO official, Abdel Harris, in Nicaragua in October 1982.[24]

In Italy two terrorist members of the Organized Automony Movement and the Red Brigades were arrested in November 1979 during an attempt to transport Soviet-made Strela missiles supplied by the Popular Front (PFLP). The two testified before an Italian court to the ties between Italian terrorists and the PLO. They said that most of the weapons in their possession were of Czech origin and supplied by the PLO.[25]

The practical implications of such ties are also evident in the PLO-IRA relationship. In December 1972 an arms shipment sent to the IRA from Cyprus by Fatah was detained at Antwerp. In November 1977 five tons of PLO hardware—mortars, rocket launchers, automatic weapons, and explosives—were intercepted in Belgium. The arms were concealed in electrical transformers en route from Cyprus to the Irish Republic for use by the IRA.

The considerable reduction in violence in Northern Ireland in 1977 has been attributed to the fact that the IRA ran short of combat matériel. Early in 1978, however, the IRA received a new supply of weapons from the Mideast. This fresh equipment enabled the IRA to initiate a new offensive.[26]

Operations

The flow of Soviet-made military hardware and the PLO operational assistance are reciprocal. The weapons found in the apartment of the international underground network, uncovered in Paris in July 1975, included hand grenades stolen from the U.S. Army depot in West Germany by members of the Baader-Meinhof Gang. The Japanese Red Army used stolen hand grenades in the raid on the French Embassy in the Hague in September 1974, and in an attack—apparently perpetrated by Carlos—on a Paris drugstore during the same month.[27]

Members of the Fatah and the Popular Front (PFLP) have provided operational support to the IRA. The assassination of the British Ambassador in the Hague in March 1979 was attributed to the PLO assassination groups.

The foreign terrorists' military payoff to the PLO has been expressed in joint operations and "proxy" attacks, as during the civil war in Jordan in September 1970. It was then that the Sandinistas fought with the PLO against King Hussein's troops. Furthermore, in exchange for the PLO's increased assistance during the past several years, political[28] and military,[29] an El Salvadoran terrorist squad kidnapped and subsequently killed South Africa's Ambassador in San Salvador in November 1979. One of the original demands of the kidnappers was for a break in El Salvador's relations with Israel and official recognition of the PLO. In the following month, another terrorist group attacked the Israeli Embassy in San Salvador "in solidarity with the Palestinian people." Again, they demanded the government to establish diplomatic ties with the PLO.[30]

Documents captured by Israeli forces in Lebanon in the summer of 1982 reveal that various Communist groups in Western and Third World nations benefited from PLO assistance, especially from its Marxist-Leninist factions, the Popular Front (PFLP) and the Democratic Front (DFLP). The documents, selected as examples of this PLO outreach, are listed and described below:

- According to a document dated June 18, 1981, eight Democratic Front (DFLP) officers, who had been trained in the Soviet Union, were subsequently sent to Iran to train members of the local Communist Party.
- A journal found in a PLO command post in Tyre relates ties with terrorist groups in Malawi, South Africa, El Salvador, Haiti, and Turkey. A June entry (year uncertain) tells about a course for "comrades" from Malawi; an entry for May 16, 1981, reports that comrades from South Africa are about to leave Lebanon; an examination in a course for Salvadoran fighters is mentioned on February 26, 1981; and a course for comrades from Haiti is cited in April.
- A series of monthly reports found in southern Lebanon detail the Popular Front's (PFLP's) contacts with the Soviet Union, Czechoslovakia, Poland, Hungary, East Germany, Cuba, and Yugoslavia with leftist organizations in Chile, Japan, Cyprus, Denmark, Turkey, Greece, Spain, and Sri Lanka. One report of June 1979 includes information on the front's talks with Marxist-Leninist groups in Greece. The two sides were in complete agreement on all topics apart from Cambodia (Kampuchea), where the Greeks regarded Vietnam as the aggressor.

- Another document concerns a visit to Lebanon by a delegation of the Danish Left Socialist Party, which had been invited by the Popular Front (PFLP). The visit, from July 27 to August 12, 1980, included a tour of the front's military bases.
- A letter written by Ahmed Jibril's Popular Front–General Command on April 15, 1980, includes a detailed program for a visit by a Portuguese Communist Party delegation to the front's bases in southern Lebanon, in Na'ama, Sarafand, Sidon, Ein Hilwe, Al-Barj Al Shamali, Tyre, and Rashidiye.
- Excerpts from the report of the International Department of the Popular Front (PFLP) for the month of June 1980 detail the following activities undertaken during the year:

  > *With the Argentinian Workers' Party:* The department hosted an Argentinian delegation for a period of six months. Members of the delegation attended joint meetings and sat in on courses to familiarize themselves with the struggle of the Palestinians. In turn, they explained the conditions of the Argentinian peoples.
  > *With the Revolutionary Front for the Restoration of East Timor's Independence:* The PLO invited a delegate representing the Revolutionary Front to visit Beirut. The group reviewed the problems of Palestine and East Timor.
  > *With the Popular Front for the Liberation of Eritrea:* The Popular Front (PFLP) met with the Eritrean representatives to exchange views and positions.

- Excerpts from the report of the Liberation Movement Department of the Popular Front (PFLP) in June 1980 reveal these additional activities:

  > In response to an invitation from the Popular Front (PFLP), the Chilean Communist Party and the Workers' and Farmers' (Leninist-Marxist) Party in Chile visited Lebanon. During their week-long stay, the two Chilean parties became acquainted at first hand with the military, information, and communal activities of the Popular Front. They discussed the political situation in South America and in the Arab world. Before leaving, the Chilean parties signed an agreement of cooperation with the Popular Front.

- Letters sent by the Liberation Movement Department indicate the Popular Front's (PFLP's) attempts to establish or maintain connections with foreign groups. Letters were addressed to the Iranian Freedom Fighters to familiarize them with the political situation in the Arab region; to the Afghans to renew an invitation to visit Beirut; to the Ethiopian Workers' Party requesting the party to strengthen ties. In addition, a telegram was sent to the founders of the Ethiopian Workers' Party.

- Interrogation records: During the summer of 1982, the Israeli forces made contact with persons suspected of being terrorists involved in the Lebanese operation. Of the 9,000 persons questioned, 2,000 were foreign nationals. Those the Israelis detained were citizens of Austria, Bangladesh, Canada, France, India, Iran, Ivory Coast, Mali, Mauritania, Niger, Nigeria, Norway, Pakistan, the Philippines, Senegal, Somalia, and Sri Lanka.

- The documents noted that the Israeli government had informed the Red Cross in October 1982 that it was prepared to release 700 foreign nationals, and many governments were reluctant to accept them. Bangladesh, for example, reported it was unwilling to cover the cost of the return voyage of some 420 of its citizens.

South Yemen as a Training Base

- In 1979 about 7,000 Cubans, supported by 1,500 Russians and 116 East Germans, trained terrorist groups from all parts of the world at three training camps in South Yemen—Hauf, Mukallah, and Al-Gheidah. Members of the West German Red Army Faction and a number of South Moluccans from the Netherlands recently visited there. In addition, another terrorist organization, the Red Resistance Front, an obscure group estimated at twelve persons, returned to the Netherlands after intensive training. It is feared that the members of this front will soon put their training into practice.[31]

- South Moluccan terrorists, who held a whole passenger train hostage in the Netherlands, received military training in South Yemen. The Moluccans also have links with African countries and with subnational groups.[32]

- "The majority of the terrorist raids in Europe start in South Yemen," according to the Italian publication *Il Settimanale*, "the tiny state at the extreme southern tip of the Arabian peninsula which is completely under the control of the Soviet Union."[33]

- A CBS television news report cites South Yemen as a major terrorist training center. Among terrorists groups that train there are German terrorists, South Moluccan terrorists, and IRA terrorists.[34]
- During a visit to Aden in mid-February 1983, the Deputy Chairman of the Soviet State Committee for Foreign Economic Relations, Vladimir Mordbinov, obtained South Yemen's agreement to enlarge the training areas allocated to the Palestine Liberation Organization. The PLO's leader, Yasser Arafat, told a committee of the Palestine National Council in Algiers at the end of February that the Aden government had agreed after some "Soviet prodding" that almost all PLO training would take place on its territory.

Sixteen experts in guerrilla warfare, seven Russians, and nine Cubans, arrived in Aden in early March 1983. Their job was to conduct three-month and five-month courses in the four main PLO training camps in South Yemen: at Dhali and Naqub (both north of Aden), at Shuqra (on the Gulf of Aden), and at Sheikh Othman, near Aden. The curriculum is said to include the handling of explosives and the preparation of improvised explosive charges; the use of infantry weapons; bridge demolition and mine-laying; the arranging of ambushes; and information-gathering.[35]

Libya's Critical Support

- *Akher Sa'a,* the semi-official Egyptian weekly magazine, has published a list of training camps maintained by Libya for training terrorists. Ten camps have been identified as follows:

    1. Al-'Aziziyya Camp (south of Tripoli): training the Polisario Front and international terrorists
    2. Al-Ma'had Camp (the name means "the institute"): training Libyan terrorists

3. Al-Sa'iqa Camp (no location given; the name means "lightning bolt"): training Africans, Palestinians, Italian Red Brigades, and members of the Basque Separatists
4. Al-Shahid Maqarief Camp: training Libyans
5. Sebha Camp West: training terrorists
6. Jaghbub Camp (at the Jaghbub or Jarabub Oasis, near Egypt): training extremist groups
7. Surt Camp (at Surt or Sirte on the Gulf of Sirte): training assassins
8. Tarhuna Camp (southeast of Tripoli): training extremist Arab groups
9. Taybmi Camp: training extremist Tunisian groups
10. Umm al-Aranib Camp (about 25 miles south of Sebha Oasis): training assassins[36]

- The Libyan Secretary of Information, Muhammad al-Zuwayy, confirmed Libya's support of terrorism. "We are proud to be used," said al-Zuwayy. "We assert to the whole world that we provide material, moral, and political support to every liberation revolution in the world."[37]
- The oil-rich Qaddafi regime in Libya has for some years been the world's most unabashed governmental proponent of revolutionary violence. The recipients of its favors (in the form of various combinations of financial, logistical, and technical support) have been numerous and varied.[38]
- Terrorists are supplied with forged passports, cash, documents, contacts, and weapons in Libya.[39]
- Libyan diplomatic pouches have been used to smuggle money and weapons to Palestinian terrorists operating in Western Europe.[40]
- Libya has sent arms, by diplomatic courier, to many revolutionary groups which engage in terrorist acts.[41]
- Terrorist organizations based in Indonesia received money and weapons from Libya. The Libyan Embassy in Kuala Lumpur, Malaysia, served as the contact point for the Asian terrorists and the Libyans.[42]
- Libya is a source of arms and money for the IRA. The IRA has

had links with Arab terrorist groups, including the Black September organization, and the Provos, an IRA faction, have been trained by Palestinians.[43]

- Colonel Qaddafi, in a speech made on June 11, 1972, announced that Libya was sending arms, money, and volunteers to help the IRA. He also said that Libya was helping Muslims in the Philippines in insurrection against that government.[44]
- Iranian terrorists received both financial support and training from Libya.[45]
- An official statement published in Iran declared that "the rebels responsible for the recent killings and clashes with the Iranian police (May 1976) received arms and funds from Libya and the PFLP." The statement goes on to say that confirmation of the relations among the Iranian rebels, Libya, and the Popular Front (PFLP) was found in confiscated documents.[46]
- Carlos has a home in Libya given to him by Libyan leader Colonel Qaddafi in gratitude for Carlos's terrorist activities.[47]
- Sandinista and Salvadoran guerrilla links with the Libyans have resulted in significant amounts of arms and training, and there have been numerous visits of Nicaraguan leaders to Libya. In May 1981, Qaddafi provided a $100-million six-month deposit to the Sandinistas which has since been renewed. The Nicaraguans have repeatedly asked—without results—for more economic assistance from Qaddafi, presumably because of Libya's poor economic situation.
- Qaddafi has concentrated his recent efforts in behalf of the Sandanista guerrillas on providing arms. Brazil's capture of four aircraft carrying Libyan arms to Nicaragua is only the latest of a series of Libyan shipments to the Sandinistas. The Brazilian press has reported that aircraft with five tons of grenades, missiles, anti-aircraft guns, radar, ammunition, and spare parts were in the shipment.
- Libyans are also providing military training for the Sandinistas and Salvadoran guerrillas.[48]
- Salvadoran guerrilla leader Cayetano Carpio returned from Libya to attend the funeral of his second-in-command in Managua in April 1983 before he too died violently.[49]

Cuba's Links with the PLO and the Soviet Union

- Following the Tricontinental Conference in Havana in 1966, Colonel Wadim Kotschergine of the KGB built a number of training camps for freedom fighters in Cuba's mountains.
- A former FALN member admitted he received his terrorist training in Cuba before being sent to the United States.[50]
- Cuba is a veteran guerrilla-terrorist training ground. In 1977 about three hundred Palestinians were reported to be training in Cuba.[51]
- Members of the Basque Separatists told Spanish police they received terrorist training from instructors who were Cuban soldiers in Algerian army camps outside Algiers.[52]
- A terrorist-turned-informant told the FBI that Cuban agents acted as advisers for a San Francisco area terrorist organization that planned an assassination plot against former President Gerald Ford and former California Governor Ronald Reagan.[53]
- The Weathermen, according to an FBI report, received aid from Cuban agents operating in the United States. The Cubans, working out of their various North American diplomatic missions, provided meeting facilities and training to Weathermen underground members.[54]
- Propaganda manuals of groups supporting the independence of Puerto Rico, according to FBI Director William H. Webster, are printed in Cuba.[55]
- The Revolutionary Coordinating Junta (JCR) is reported to work closely with Cuba, which has provided facilities for military training as well as funds. Security services have established that communications with Cuba are maintained by "letter boxes" in Hamburg and Milan as well as Paris.[56]
- The JCR's chief commanding officer in Europe is reported to be Fernando Luis Alvarez, who is married to Ana Maria Guevara, sister of one of the most famous Latin American revolutionary figures, Ché Guevara.
- The JCR is composed of Argentina's Revolutionary Army (ERP), Bolivia's National Liberation Army (ELN), Chile's Movement of the Revolutionary Left (MLR), Paraguay's Na-

tional Liberation Front (Frepalina), and remnants of Uruguay's National Liberation Movement (MLN/Tupamaros).

- Cuba has provided training facilities for urban terrorists and guerrillas.[57]
- The M-19, a group closely allied with the JCR and composed of Dominicans who promote themselves as champions of the working classes, took over the U.S. Embassy in Colombia about noon on April 14, 1980. Once the action became known, it was quickly noted that the Soviet Ambassador to Colombia and envoys from other Communist bloc nations had arrived early and excused themselves only minutes before the M-19 forces appeared on the scene. "They certainly gave the impression that they knew something that the rest of us didn't know," one diplomat mused.[58]
- Castro provided safe haven and support to Nicaraguan leftists for almost twenty years, and the Sandinistas are indebted to him.[59]
- The Cubans provided about 2,000 teachers, military, and technical personnel within six months after the Sandinistas came to power in Nicaragua. The Cuban presence in Nicaragua has now grown to about 6,000 civilians and between 1,500 and 2,000 military and security personnel. In addition, Cubans are providing military and other training to Nicaraguans in Cuba. Cuban advisers are present with every Nicaraguan military unit. At Salvadoran guerrilla headquarters near Managua, Cuban officers join Sandinista commanders and Salvadoran guerrilla leaders in providing advice to the guerrillas in the field on tactics, targets, and communications.[60]
- Castro appointed Julio Diaz, a Cuban intelligence operative and adviser to the Sandinistas during the 1979 war, as Ambassador to Nicaragua.[61]
- The Sandinista military forces, with thirty-six new installations under construction since 1979, are being reorganized along Cuban lines.[62]
- In summarizing the Cuban link with the Soviet Union, Senator Jeremiah Denton, Chairman of the Subcommittee on Security and Terrorism of the Senate Committee on the Judiciary stated on April 30, 1983, "The Soviets seem to direct certain Cuban

activities and have assigned the United States as their ultimate number one target. Cuban operations include participating in the support of low intensity warfare and terrorist activity which is designed to destabilize and extend Soviet/Cuban influence in the region by destroying existing governments and replacing them with Soviet puppets. . . . Some of this activity may not be definitely directed by the Soviet Union, but it is certainly supported by them."[63]

The infrastructure of terrorism in Soviet surrogate states has greatly facilitated Soviet wars of national liberation. Partially as a result, a total of thirty-one nations—peoples with a strong sense of cultural identity, ethnic solidarity, and common language—have become captive within the Soviet sphere of political and military domination. Of these Cuba, South Vietnam, Kampuchea, and Afghanistan have fallen since 1961, when Khrushchev praised Fidel Castro for establishing a Marxist regime, the first in the Americas in the Soviet bloc. Castro has been a faithful protégé of the Soviet Union ever since then, almost a quarter of a century.

Chapter 6

The United States Confronts Wars of National Liberation

The 1980s present a grave challenge to the future of U.S. national security, economic well-being, and the political processes of representative government in an open society. Political oppression and outright captivity are widespread in our troubled time.

Sovereign states should have the right to settle on their own form of government and international alignments free from the coercion of externally supported wars of national liberation. Free people are not predestined to bow forever to the kind of tyranny that has dominated so much of the world for such long periods from the time of the Chin Dynasty to Genghis Khan and Joseph Stalin.

The toughness of the urge for freedom under adversity is demonstrated today by the courageous workers of Poland, virtually abandoned by Western nations to Soviet military occupation and political oppression over three decades ago. The power of spiritual and moral forces in opposition to guns and bayonets is illustrated by the words and actions of the Polish Pope, John Paul II.

Only now are political leaders and intellectuals in the non-Communist world learning that the Soviet term "war of national liberation" is simply Leninist double-talk for a conflict that destabilizes nations cooperating with the United States. For this reason the United States, the ultimate target, faces a persistent hostile Soviet behavior pattern of aggression below the level of nuclear war, often below the level of what is recognized as war of any kind.

Americans congenitally hope for a stable international environment that facilitates peaceful solution of problems. They are often inclined to wishful thinking, expecting the best against impossible odds. Their great temptation, obvious in the 1970s, was provocative weakness. On the contrary, the leaders of militant Communist nations seek to exploit indigenous difficulties in other nations, to disrupt social order, and to promote Communist revolutions, alternately threatening and cajoling everyone who resisted.

The endgame is political: control of people, territory, resources, and technology. Conflicts over these assets of modern national power are bound to be severe and widespread for a long time.

The Strategy of the Soviet Union

It is still the strategy of the leaders of the Soviet Union to increase and expand the reach of their power, neutralizing U.S. military capabilities with the threat of nuclear war implicit in the gigantic Soviet military weapons buildup of the 1970s. The Soviet aim is to destroy the political will of all non-Communist nations to pay the price of adequate regional self-defense.

The Soviet strategy, long-established and well understood by the Communist Party leaders, is to win concessions from weak and fearful foreign governments without actually waging wars that would damage the economic infrastructure whose output they covet. Soviet leaders believe in the maxim enunciated by their onetime Chinese comrade, Mao Tse-tung, that political power grows from the barrel of a gun. They want to dominate and exploit the resources and the technology of the world. They have no fixed timetable.

Stalin in his own heyday hoped for exactly this achievement. He made a mighty surge forward in both East Europe and Northeast Asia, but failed to detach either Germany or Japan from a friendly relationship with the United States.

At best, the turbulence and violence created by the Soviet leaders since World War II are merely containable for the next few years. Some situations at worst could start a landslide that would be irreversible, forcing the United States to take measures that would unavoidably disrupt the peaceful, consumer-oriented American way of life.

The Soviet Union gains considerable psychological benefits in a conflict environment that tends to push pluralist states to compromise, accommodation, or outright appeasement. In contrast, members of the Soviet Politburo are able to bargain hard, take risks, and play to win. Neither Soviet public opinion nor the Soviet information media is a bar to their risk-taking. This fact encourages the Soviets to resort to terrorism, guerrilla warfare, and "wars of national liberation" when these serve their geopolitical interests. All these soften the social fabric and political resolve of the states they target as adversaries.

Political revolutionary activity, as carried out by the Communist world with terrorism as a primary tool, is a ubiquitous threat. As a result in many areas—particularly now in the Mideast, Central Africa, and the Caribbean—Soviet propaganda, weapons, and proxy police and military forces from East Germany and Cuba feed the fires of conflict. They are fanned and kept hot by the PLO and its associates in sabotage and war.

The U.S. Response to Confrontation

When President John F. Kennedy came into office in 1960 he noted that the Soviet Union, abiding by the doctrine that wars of national liberation were fair game, could create and support what he called bushfire wars anywhere. He intervened first in Laos and later in Vietnam because he feared the bushfire wars there would spread out of control and shift the balance of power in favor of the Communist world. He foresaw that ultimately such undeclared low-intensity wars—what he called "long twilight struggles"—could isolate the United States from its international sources of political and economic strength. Then the United States would be inferior in strategic power and outreach to the expanding Soviet empire, perhaps aided out of a sense of expediency by the People's Republic of China (PRC).

In the outcome, President Kennedy's fears proved to be well founded. Americans were psychologically ill-prepared to wage a long but limited unconventional war in the jungles of Southeast Asia. In a climate of fractured consensus at home, Presidents Lyndon Johnson and Richard Nixon began to search for ways to withdraw the U.S. forces and in the spirit of détente to ease tensions between Moscow and Washington. The result was the final U.S. abandonment of South Vietnam and its absorption by the Communist state, whose government, based in Hanoi, assumed power in 1954.

Even after President Kennedy went to the brink of war to keep Soviet nuclear weapons out of Cuba, the United States thereafter acquiesced when the Soviets persisted in building a major military stronghold on the island. Castro, a faithful follower of the Soviet Union for a quarter of a century, has exported terrorists, soldiers, and guns whenever and wherever the Kremlin bids.

The United States has not found a remedy for wars of national liberation. Unless it does, the Vietnam tragedy will be repeated and the Soviet-Cuban model government now on the doorstep of the United States will spread. The Reagan administration is awakening to these facts, perhaps slowly and with uncertain public support.

The Formula for Wars of National Liberation

The formula for wars of national liberation is simple. First, the Soviet Union acquires a political base for expansion in a region where its strategic ambitions lie. Then it sends Soviet advisers, weapons, money, and political propaganda. The Cubans provide troops for local security and tactical military training, as they have in Latin America, Africa, and the Mideast. The East Germans send trainers and advisers for intelligence services. In Southeast Asia, Vietnam does military proxy work.

When indigenous splinter minorities take their perennial battles for political power into the jungles and streets, the Soviets, Cubans, East Germans, or Vietnamese, and sometimes the Chinese, are there with weapons, funds, and training. Their role is to settle problems of economic discontent with violence in the name of Communist goals. With this support, the more militant faction almost always ends up victorious in the revolutionary movement, and if the revolution succeeds, Moscow gains control of the nation.

This process may not be well described as dominoes falling, but it has been clear now for more than two decades that it is a recipe for destruction of open societies trying to establish pluralist political freedoms.

U.S. Strategy

The net result is that the United States needs to adopt a strategy of flatly denouncing and strategically countering expansionist political "liberation" moves by Communist totalitarian states wherever they are in process.

In this field of low-intensity conflict the United States should focus the skills of its conventional military forces and such covert-action intelligence work as are needed to counter Soviet-sponsored forward thrusts. Such efforts are strategically defensive—not provocative as is often alleged. They serve freedom and self-determination, basic concepts in the political value system of the United States. They must be undertaken vigorously and with technical virtuosity if the tide is to be turned in the ongoing wars of national liberation where vital U.S. interests are at stake.

While El Salvador, Honduras, Costa Rica, and Guatemala are not significant factors in regional power politics, Mexico and Panama are. Destabilization of this whole region would be the most meaningful strategic defeat the Soviet Union could inflict on the United States today.

Such a Central American debacle has the potential of starting the avalanche of political despair and changing strategic alignments that would tilt the balance of world power toward U.S. inferiority that would be virtually irreversible except by a major war.

The next fallback positions may be impossible to defend if the too-little, too-late syndrome in U.S. strategic policy vindicates Nicaraguan policies and permits El Salvador to succumb to the Soviet-Cuban model of dictatorial government.

Soviet head of state Yuri Andropov has made his views clear over many years. In 1970 he said, "The fraternal socialist countries are not simply a sum total of states, but a sociopolitical and economic community."[1] In the same doctrinal speech he added, "[Soviet] policy in relation to the national liberation movement is well known," emphasizing "the necessity of all-round support for the peoples fighting against imperialism."

In 1979 Andropov expanded these declarations with the statement that favorable changes were taking place in Angola, Afghanistan, Kampuchea, and Iran. He said, "Nothing, absolutely nothing, can stop the irresistible forces of history." In 1983, with leaders of the Soviet bloc, he denounced the Israeli and U.S. role in Lebanon, commended efforts at "establishing a new international economic order and ensuring the complete sovereignty of countries in Asia, Latin America, and Oceania over their natural resources," and warned that "an end should be put to the [U.S.] policy of continuous threats and provocations against Cuba and Nicaragua."[2]

In view of Soviet doctrines along these lines and the sorry record of PLO, Cuban, and other terrorist activities, the most urgent task of all for the United States in the troubled world of the 1980s is to find the way and the will to stop wars of national liberation.

A full-scale strategic U.S. counterattack to suppress the tremendously destructive bushfire wars of national liberation, supported externally by Communist states, might return some order and hope to the worst conflict zones of the globe.

The big-power relationships involving Moscow, Peking, and Washington could only improve in the atmosphere of reduced hostility that would result from U.S. victories in demonstrating that bushfire wars do not pay off in political plums for totalitarian style governments.

The end goal, entirely in keeping with mainstream American principles of political liberty and morality, would be the positive international achievement of increased chances for freedom and self-determination.

Appendix: A Selection of PLO Documents Found in Lebanon, June 1982

Document I. Protocol of Talks Between PLO and Soviet Delegations in Moscow

THE MEETING TOOK PLACE IN THE KREMLIN ON 13 NOVEMBER 1979 AT 1200 HRS.

PARTICIPANTS:-

<u>SOVIET DELEGATION</u>

SOVIET FOREIGN MINISTER GROMYKO

PONOAMAREV,GROMYKO'S DEPUTY

GRINEVSKY, HEAD OF MIDDLE EAST DEPARTMENT
IN SOVIET FOREIGN OFFICE

<u>PLO DELEGATION</u>

ABU AMER (YASSER ARAFAT)

ABED EL MAHSIN ABU MEIZER
(MEMBER OF PLO EXECUTIVE COMMITTEE)

TLAL NAJI (JIBRIL FRONT, MEMBER
OF PLO EXECUTIVE COMMITTEE)

AZAM ALKACHI (SA'AQA)

YASSER ABED RABAH (DEMOCRATIC
FRONT, MEMBER OF PLO EXECUTIVE
COMMITTEE)

HABIB KAHWAJI (SA'AQA, MEMBER OF
PLO EXECUTIVE COMMITTEE)

TAISIR KABAH (POPULAR FRONT/HABASH)

MUHAMED AL SHA'ER (PLO REPRESENTA-
TIVE IN THE USSR)

ABED EL RAHIM AHMED (ARAB
LIBERATION FRONT)

NOTE: Original text in Arabic;
   TRANSLATOR'S REMARKS ARE IN BRACKETS

GROMYKO: I WELCOME YOU ON BEHALF OF THE SOVIET LEADERSHIP, ON BEHALF OF
BREZHNEV AND PERSONALLY UPON YOUR ARRIVAL IN MOSCOW. THE SOVIET LEADER-
SHIP APPOINTED ME AND PONOAMAREV TO DISCUSS WITH YOU ALL THE PROBLEMS
OF INTEREST TO YOU AND TO US. I ASK YOU TO REGARD THIS AS YOUR POINT OF
DEPARTURE, AS I HAVE NO SUBJECT TO RAISE JUST NOW.

I HOPE OUR MEETING WILL BE IN A SPIRIT OF FRIENDSHIP AND LOVE, AS WERE
OUR PREVIOUS MEETINGS. I SUGGEST, FOR THE PURPOSE OF BEGINNING THE TALKS,
THAT YOU TELL US YOUR OPINIONS AND AT A LATER STAGE WE WILL PRESENT OURS.
AFTERWARDS, LUNCH WILL BE SERVED - TODAY AT 2 O'CLOCK.

ABU AMER: I WILL BE BRIEF, SINCE ONE OF THE COMRADES TOLD ME THAT THIS
PERIOD OF TIME WAS INTENDED FOR FORMAL TALKS.

GROMYKO: WE HAVE PLENTY OF TIME ...

ABU AMER: TWO HOURS ARE NOT ENOUGH.

GROMYKO: TWO AND A HALF ...

ABU AMER: WE HAVE NOT TALKED TOGETHER FOR A LONG TIME. BEFORE THE BAGHDAD
CONFERENCE I TOLD YOU THAT IT WOULD BE AMONG THE MOST IMPORTANT SUMMITS
AND ITS RESULTS WERE IN FACT IMPORTANT AS I EXPECTED. THIS WAS SO SINCE
THE BAGHDAD SUMMIT PUT THE ARAB NATION AS A WHOLE AGAINST THE "CAMP
DAVID COMBINATION", EXCEPT FOR TWO STATES. YOU UNDOUBTEDLY KNOW THE DECI-
SIONS OF THE BAGHDAD SUMMIT. (THEREFORE) I DO NOT "JUMP" TO TALK
ABOUT THE ARAB FOREIGN AND ECONOMIC MINISTERS SUMMIT.

THE IMPORTANCE OF BAGHDAD IS THAT THE ARABS MET WITHOUT SADAT, WHO DECLARED
THAT THE ARABS COULD NOT HAVE A SUMMIT WITHOUT HIM. (IN BAGHDAD) DECISIONS
WERE MADE WHICH CONDEMN THE CAMP DAVID ACCORDS.

THE MEETING OF THE FOREIGN AND ECONOMIC MINISTERS WAS MORE IMPORTANT
BECAUSE ITS DECISIONS WERE DECISIONS FOR IMPLEMENTATION OF THE (PREVIOUS)
DECISIONS OF THE POLITICAL SUMMIT (IN BAGHDAD)...
AND AS YOU KNOW, ~~BZEZHINSKI~~ BRZEZINSKI CARRIED OUT A VISIT IN THE REGION AND ANNOUNCED
THAT THE PURPOSE OF HIS VISIT WAS TO PREVENT THE IMPLEMENTATION OF THE
DECISIONS OF THE BAGHDAD CONFERENCE.

GROMYKO: DO YOU REFER TO HIS LAST TRIP? (OF BŽEZHINSKI)

ABU AMER: (I REFER) TO THE TRIP WHICH PRECEDED THE MEETING OF THE ARAB FOREIGN
AND ECONOMIC MINISTERS. THE IMPORTANCE OF THE SECOND BAGHDAD SUMMIT -
THE ARAB FOREIGN AND ECONOMIC MINISTERS - WAS IN THE COORDINATION WHICH
FOUND EXPRESSION IN THE FORM OF A (POLITICAL) TRIPARTITE AXIS BETWEEN
IRAQ,SYRIA AND PALESTINE. THIS AXIS LED THE (BLOCK OF THE) "STEADFASTNESS
FRONT" AND LATER DIRECTED THE COURSE OF THE ENTIRE CONFERENCE.

THESE DECISIONS WERE TAKEN AND I REGARD THEM AS ECONOMIC DECISIONS - WHICH
ARE MORE IMPORTANT THAN THE POLITICAL DECISIONS (TAKEN AT THE PREVIOUS
SUMMIT). AND WE CAN SAY THAT THE PALESTINIAN DELEGATION PLAYED AN
IMPORTANT ROLE IN MAKING THESE DECISIONS.

GROMYKO: COMRADE ARAFAT, FORGIVE ME FOR INTERRUPTING YOU BUT I ASK YOU TO
EXPRESS YOUR OPINION ABOUT THE EXTENT TO WHICH THE DECISIONS TAKEN AT THE
BAGHDAD CONFERENCE WERE IMPLEMENTED.

ABU AMER: THAT IS PRECISELY WHAT I AM ABOUT TO TALK ABOUT. SOME OF THE
ARABS WANTED TO PROVIDE US WITH A POLITICAL DECISION AND (SIMULTANEOUSLY)
MANIPULATE (ON THEIR PART) THE ECONOMIC DECISIONS. THE PALESTINIAN
DELEGATION SUBMITTED (TO THE COMMITTEE) A CLEAR ECONOMIC (WORKING)PAPER,
WHICH WAS SUPPORTED BY THE TWO DELEGATIONS OF SYRIA AND IRAQ. (AND SO) A
WONDERFUL COORDINATION WAS CREATED BETWEEN US (PLO, IRAQ AND SYRIA) SO THAT
WE COULD STAND AGAINST THE BLOC WHICH WAS LED BY SAUDI ARABIA. THIS TURNED THE
WHOLE MEETING INTO A KIND OF SUMMIT CONFERENCE. THEN WE CAUSED
THE ADJOURNMENT OF THE SUMMIT FOR 48 HOURS TO ENABLE ALL THE DELEGATES TO
RETURN TO THEIR COUNTRIES FOR CONSULTATIONS. HERE I WOULD LIKE TO REPEAT AND
STRESS THE IMPORTANCE OF THE TRIPARTITE COORDINATION WHICH PLAYED A DECISIVE
ROLE IN THE SUCCESS OF THE SUMMIT AND WHICH BROUGHT ABOUT THE RESULTS YOU
KNOW ABOUT.

AS REGARDS THE ECONOMIC DECISIONS, IT IS FAIR TO SAY THAT AGAINST EGYPT
ABOUT 90% WERE IMPLEMENTED. I SAY 90% SINCE 10% OF THE DEPOSITS HAVE
STILL NOT BEEN WITHDRAWN (FROM EGYPTIAN BANKS). NOW KAMAL ADHAM

THIS WAS YOUR ESTIMATE, TOO. NOW I HAVE NO CHOICE BUT TO MENTION THE
FACT THAT PRIOR TO THE CONFERENCE AT HAVANA THERE HAD BEEN A SHARP
DISAGREEMENT BETWEEN SYRIA AND IRAQ. BUT THE PALESTINIAN DELEGATION PLAYED
AN IMPORTANT ROLE IN COORDINATING THE TRIPARTITE POSITION, AS WE HAD DONE
IN THE BAGHDAD CONFERENCE. THE TWO PRESIDENTS, SADAM HUSSEIN AND ASSAD
PLAYED AN IMPORTANT AND CENTRAL ROLE IN THE ANTI-CAMP DAVID DECISION -
MAKING IN HAVANA. THROUGH THIS MAGNIFICENT TRIPARTITE COORDINATION AND
DUE TO THE ROLE COMRADE CASTRO PLAYED - WHOM WE SHALL NOT FORGET - WE
SUCCEEDED IN CONSTRUCTING A MASSIVE "ALIBI" BY WHICH WE ACHIEVED THOSE WELL-
KNOWN DECISIONS.

PONOAMAREV: THE CUBAN COMRADES PLAYED AN ENORMOUS ROLE.

ABU AMER: CASTRO'S WISDOM PLAYED AN IMPORTANT ROLE CONCERNING THE RESULTS.
ONE SHOULD ALSO MENTION HERE THE ROLE OF THE MANY PROGRESSIVE COUNTRIES THAT
WERE OF CONSIDERABLE HELP TO US. I WILL PROCEED TO TALK (NOW) ABOUT THE
LISBON CONGRESS, WHICH IS NO LESS IMPORTANT THAN THE HAVANA CONGRESS.
WHILE THE FORMER WAS A POPULAR CONGRESS, THE LATTER WAS A CONGRESS OF GOVERNMENTS.
IT WAS ONE OF THOSE WONDERFUL POPULAR CONGRESSES AND IT WAS THE FIRST
TO BE HELD IN A EUROPEAN COUNTRY. THE PORTUGESE COMMUNIST PARTY PLAYED
AN IMPORTANT ROLE TO ENSURE ITS SUCCESS AND SO DID YOUR "SOLIDARITY
COMMITTEE".

PONOAMAREV: WE SENT (THERE) THE HEAD OF THE SOLIDARITY COMMITTEE, AND
COMRADE BREZHNEV SENT A MESSAGE TO THE CONGRESS.

ABU AMER: RIGHT. THERE WERE MANY LETTERS FROM KINGS AND PRESIDENTS AT THE
HEAD OF WHICH WAS THAT OF COMRADE BREZHNEV. THE BARCELONA (SUMMIT) WAS
A TURNING-POINT (TOWARDS US) IN THE WESTERN WORLD. NOW, I WISH TO SAY
THAT AFTER OUR SUCCESS IN THE FIRST AND SECOND BAGHDAD CONFERENCES, AN
AMERICAN COUNTER-ATTACK WAS LAUNCHED IN THE FOLLOWING AXES:

THE FIRST AXIS: A PLOT WAS PUT INTO ACTION WHICH SEPARATED IRAQ FROM SYRIA,
AND INTERNAL PROBLEMS OCCURRED IN SYRIA. IN ADDITION PRESSURE WAS PUT
ON KING HUSSEIN TO JOIN CAMP DAVID. FURTHERMORE, THERE WAS THE AMERICAN
SHOW OF STRENGTH IN THE (PERSIAN) GULF.

I MUST ADMIT, THE SHOW OF STRENGTH IN THE GULF WAS SUCCESSFUL.
AN ATTEMPT WAS ALSO MADE TO SEPARATE THE IRANIAN REVOLUTION FROM
THE ARABS.

THE SECOND AXIS: (INCLUDED THE) PRESSURE ON OUR PEOPLE IN THE
TERRITORIES TO COOPERATE WITH THE AUTONOMY (PLAN). ONE MUST SAY,THEY
FAILED IN THIS (AND THE PROOF OF THIS IS) THAT STRAUSS, THE ISRAELIS
AND THE EGYPTIANS ADMITTED IT. NOW OUR OCCUPIED LAND IS IN TURMOIL WITH
MASS STRIKES BECAUSE OF ISRAEL'S DECISION TO EXILE ONE OF THE MAYORS
(BASSAM SHAK'A) BECAUSE HE WAS A PLO MEMBER AND SINCE THERE IS A DECISION
TO GET RID OF THEM (THE MAYORS) ONE BY ONE.

WE HAVE TO ADMIT THAT THE TALKS HELD BETWEEN BURG AND MUSTAFA HALIL
RESULTED IN HALIL'S AGREEMENT, ACCORDING TO SADAT'S INSTRUCTIONS, TO THE
AUTONOMY PLAN. SO THEY REACHED SOME ALMOST-FINAL AGREEMENTS EXCEPT FOR JERU-
SALEM, STATE LANDS AND THE NATURAL RESOURCES. THESE SUBJECTS WERE LEFT FOR
A LATER DATE.

THE THIRD AXIS:(THE ISRAELIS) HAVE CONCENTRATED ON US (MILITARILY), A
CONCENTRATION THAT IS CLOSE TO HELL IN SOUTH LEBANON.
SEVEN MONTHS OF HELL CREATED 600,000 LEBANESE AND PALESTINIANS HOMELESS
AND LEFT TENS OF CITIES, VILLAGES AND REFUGEE CAMPS DESTROYED. FOR THIS
PURPOSE ISRAEL USED ALL TYPES OF ARMS IN ITS POSSESSION.

GROMYKO: 600,000 LEBANESE AND PALESTINIAN EMMIGRANTS FROM THE SOUTH TO THE
NORTH? WHEN DID THE WAR AGAINST YOU START?

ABU AMER: SINCE THE 9TH OF MARCH 1978. I WILL GIVE YOU AN EXAMPLE OF THE
VIOLENCE OF THE WAR AGAINST US: ISRAEL SHELLED THE "RASHIDIYA" AND
"NAHER-AL-BARED" CAMPS WITH NAVAL TORPEDOES NAMED "SMART". THESE ARE GUIDED
TORPEDOES FIRED FROM THE SEA. BUT THEY DO NOT NEED THESE WEAPONS TO ATTACK US IN
THE SOUTH, SINCE THEIR ARTILLERY IS CAPABLE OF REACHING (ALL) THE TARGETS THEY ARE
INTERESTED IN.

ONCE SOME OF MY OFFICERS ASKED ME: WHAT IS THE REASON FOR THE USE OF THESE
WEAPONS (BY THE ISRAELIS)?

I REPLIED, THEY (ISRAELIS) GAVE INSTRUCTIONS TO SHOOT WITH ALL WEAPONS. SO
THE ISRAELI NAVY BOMBARDED US WITH THESE WEAPONS, WITH F-15 AND F-16 AND ALSO
"LANCE" MISSILES WERE USED AGAINST US, WHICH ARE SIMILAR TO "FROG" AND "LUNA"
MISSILES.

I HAVE THE TESTIMONY OF RAMSEY CLARK. AFTER HIS VISIT TO OUR REGION CLARK
RETURNED TO THE U.S. AND CONVENED A PRESS CONFERENCE. HE SAID THAT WHAT HAPPENED I
LEBANON WAS A CRIME. THE IMPORTANCE OF HIS TESTIMONY IS THAT HE IS ONE OF
THEM. HE VISITED THE NABATIYA CAMP WHICH WAS WIPED OUT AND ONLY 11 (UNDAMAGED)
HOUSES WERE LEFT. THEY BOMBARDED IT WITH AMMUNITION FORBIDDEN FOR USE
ACCORDING TO INTERNATIONAL LAW SUCH AS: GAS AND FRAGMENTATION BOMBS AND
"CLUSTER BOMBS". WE FOUGHT ALONE AND STILL DO SO AND WE DO NOT RECEIVE ANY
SINGLE BULLET EXCEPT FROM THE IRAQI AND SYRIAN BROTHERS WHO CLASHED TWICE WITH
THE ISRAELI AIR FORCE.

GROMYKO: HOW DO YOU EVALUATE THE RESULTS OF THE SYRIAN-ISRAELI AIR COMBAT?

ABU AMER: I'M NO AVIATION EXPERT. WHAT INTERESTS ME ARE THE POLITICAL DECISIONS.
WHAT MATTERS TO ME IS THAT OUR FIGHTER SHOULD NOT FEEL HE IS (STANDING) ALONE.

PONOAMAREV: WHAT IS IMPORTANT IS THAT THEY (THE ISRAELIS) HAVE NOT SUCCEEDED
IN BREAKING YOUR STEADFASTNESS AND YOUR (ABILITY) TO ENDURE.

ABU AMER: WHAT HAPPENED (THERE) WAS A WAR AND ONLY BY A MIRACLE DID WE SUCCEED
IN BEARING (ON OUR SHOULDERS) ALSO THE BURDEN OF FEEDING THE HOMELESS, SINCE
THERE WAS NO GOVERNMENT (WHICH COULD DO IT). WE FEED ABOUT 50% OF THEM BECAUSE
THE PURPOSE OF THE (ISRAELI) OPERATION BY THESE BARBARIC BOMBARDMENTS WAS TO
CONSOLIDATE THE MASSES OF SOUTH LEBANON AGAINST US.

THE ARAB STATES CANNOT ENDURE A WAR(OF ATTRITION). ABD EL NASSER, FOR INSTANCE
BECAME TIRED OF THE (WAR OF) ATTRITION. AND YOU REMEMBER HOW THIS
FATIGUE WAS ONE OF THE REASONS WHY HE (AGREED) TO ACCEPT THE ROGERS PLAN.

WE SAY: THERE HAVE BEEN SEVEN MONTHS (OF SUFFERING IN THE SOUTH) BUT WE ARE
READY FOR SEVENTY MONTHS AND MORE. OUR CHILDREN ARE FIGHTING AND WE DO NOT
DEMAND MORE. YESTERDAY MORNING A CLUSTER BOMB EXPLODED AND KILLED
SEVEN OF OUR CHILDREN. UNTIL NOW I DID NOT ANNOUNCE MY MILITARY LOSSES. WE
HAVE DAILY 10-12 MILITARY CAUSALTIES. AS REGARDS CIVILIAN (CASUALTIES) THE
NUMBER REACHED 30-35 A DAY. ONE MONTH AL HUS (LEBANESE PRIME MINISTER)

COUNTED 390 CIVILIANS DEAD AND 1000 WOUNDED WHO REACHED HOSPITALS,
THOUGH PROBABLY THERE ARE MORE. THESE ARE THE DIRECTIONS OF THE (AMERICAN)
ATTACK. IT HASN'T STOPPED YET, WHY? THIS HELL IN THE SOUTH IS WEAKER
NOW DUE TO AN AMERICAN WORKING PAPER SUBMITTED BY PHILIP HABIB. I WILL
GIVE YOU A COPY OF IT SO WE WILL NOT WASTE TIME. THE MOST DANGEROUS
AMONG THE STATEMENTS IN THE PAPER IS THAT THEY SPEAK ABOUT CONVENING ALL
THE PARTIES (IN THE CONFLICT) AND THEY ALSO STATE THAT THIS RELATES
TO ISRAEL, LEBANON, SYRIA, JORDAN AND THE PLO UNDER THE SUPERVISION
OF THE USA. WHY JORDAN?

PONOAMAREV: WITHOUT EGYPT?

ABU AMER: WITHOUT EGYPT. THIS IS A NEW CAMP DAVID AND THIS IS THE MOST
DANGEROUS ITEM IN THE WORKING PAPER. HERE THE SERIOUSNESS OF THE NEXT
SUMMIT IS REFLECTED. THE SERIOUSNESS RESULTS FROM THE FACT THAT A
FEW ARAB SIDES AGREED TO IT AND ACTED IN ORDER TO IMPLEMENT IT WHETHER ON
PURPOSE OR NOT. THE LEBANESE ARE ABOUT TO SUBMIT A WORKING PAPER WHICH
WILL BLOW UP THE WHOLE CONFERENCE. THE ESSENCE OF THIS PAPER IS: THE
EVACUATION OF THE PALESTINIANS FROM THE SOUTH. THE SERIOUSNESS OF THIS
PAPER IS NOT BECAUSE OF THE EXPULSION OF THE PALESTINIANS FROM THE SOUTH,
BUT BECAUSE OF TWO POINTS:

1. THIS IS A MINE WHICH WILL EXPLODE IN THE SUMMIT. THEREFORE THE SUMMIT
    WILL END IN FAILURE. A FEW ARAB STATES WILL FREE THEMSELVES OF THE
    COMMITMENTS THEY UNDERTOOK IN BAGHDAD.

2. IF THE LEBANESE WILL NOT OBTAIN THEIR GOALS IN THE CONFERENCE,
    THEY WILL TURN TO INTERNATIONALIZATION (OF THE LEBANESE PROBLEM).

WE ACHIEVED SUCCESS REGARDING THE STAGES OF THE NEXT SUMMIT. DURING MY
LAST VISIT TO BAGHDAD I REACHED AN AGREEMENT WITH PRESIDENT SADAM CONCERNING
THE TRIPARTITE COORDINATION, AS HAPPENED IN THE LAST CONFERENCE ; THIS CAN BE
CONSIDERED A SUCCESS. SADAM TOLD ME THAT THE PALESTINIANS HAVE PRIORITY IN
EVERYTHING.

ON MY RETURN I MET WITH PRESIDENT ASSAD AND I TOLD HIM ABOUT THIS. HE
WAS HAPPY ABOUT IT AND AGREED TO THIS TRIPARTITE COORDINATION. THIS IS VERY
IMPORTANT SINCE IT WILL LIMIT THE FREEDOM OF MANEUVER OF THE HOSTILE FORCES
IN THE CONFERENCE, AND THIS IS WHAT WE AGREED ABOUT IN THE STEADFASTNESS FRONT
SUMMIT DURING OUR SINGLE MEETING IN ALGERIA.

I HAVE TO ADD A FOURTH AXIS OF THE AMERICAN COUNTER-ATTACK: IT IS EXPRESSED
IN THE DEPLOYMENT OF TWO EGYPTIAN DIVISIONS ALONG THE LIBYAN BORDER IN
ORDER TO PUT AMERICAN-EGYPTIAN MILITARY PRESSURE ON MUAMMAR. THEY
SAY THAT THEY DO NOT NEED THE CONQUEST OF LIBYA, BUT ONLY TO REACH TOBRUK.
THIS MEANS TAKING CONTROL OF THE OIL WELLS AND THE ESTABLISHMENT OF A LIBYAN
GOVERNMENT BASED ON THE OPPOSITION FORCES THAT HAVE BEGUN TO ORGANIZE
(IN EGYPT). WE MUST NOT UNDERESTIMATE IT, DESPITE THE BIG PARADE KADDAFI
PRESENTED ON SEPTEMBER 1. I MUST STATE THAT THIS PRESSURE INFLUENCED THE
LIBYAN POLITICAL POSITION SLIGHTLY AND THIS IS THE REASON FOR THE VISIT OF
NEWSOM, THE AMERICAN STATE DEPARTMENT DIRECTOR FOR AFRICAN AFFAIRS IN LIBYA.

THE FIFTH AXIS FOR THE AMERICAN COUNTER ATTACK IS THE ENCOURAGEMENT OF THE
EGYPTIAN REGIME TO SUPPLY ARMS AND AMMUNITION - AND POSSIBLY FORCES TOO -
TO THE KING OF MOROCCO. THIS MEANS THE RETURN OF THE KING TO THE CAMP DAVID GROUP
BY EXPLOITING THE DEFEATS HE SUFFERED IN THE DESERT. THEREFORE WE WENT ABOUT
A MONTH AGO TO MOROCCO AND ALGERIA AND ACHIEVED GOOD RESULTS. WE RECEIVED
FROM KING HASSAN, AFTER A THREE AND A HALF HOUR MEETING, HIS CONSENT FOR A
REFERENDUM. THIS IS AN IMPORTANT POLITICAL ACHIEVEMENT THAT WE GAINED IN
NORTH AFRICA. I RETURNED LATER TO ALGERIA AND INFORMED PRESIDENT SHADLI
ABOUT THE MATTER. A FEW DAYS AGO I INFORMED THE POLISARIO LEADERS
ABOUT IT AND WE AWAIT THEIR REPLY.

PONOAMAREV: WHAT DO YOU MEAN BY A REFERENDUM? A DISENGAGEMENT OF FORCES?

ABU AMER: SELF DETERMINATION TO THE INHABITANTS OF THE DESERT.

GROMYKO: DO BOTH SIDES AGREE TO A REFERENDUM?

ABU AMER: THE KING OF MOROCCO AGREED AND I AWAIT THE REPLY OF THE ALGERIANS
AND OF THE POLISARIO LEADERS. REGARDING THE COUNTER-ATTACK, THERE WAS A
CONFERENCE WHICH WAS ONE OF THE MOST SEVERE ONES. THIS CONFERENCE OF THE FOREIGN
MINISTERS OF THE GULF STATES AND SAUDI ARABIA DISCUSSED THE SECURITY
OF THE GULF. IRAQ IS LOCATED IN THE GULF AND THE QUESTION IS: WHY WAS IT
NOT INVITED TO THE CONFERENCE. THE MAIN SUBJECT ON THE AGENDA, ACCORDING
TO THEM, WAS THE PALESTINIAN - IRANIAN ALLIANCE AND THE DANGER IT PRESENTS TO
THEM. THEY MADE PLANS TO COPE WITH THIS SUBJECT, WHICH EXISTS ONLY IN THEIR
IMAGINATION.

WE SUCCEEDED IN ESCALATING MILITARY ACTIVITIES IN THE OCCUPIED TERRITORIES.
IT IS ENOUGH TO POINT TO THE REPORT OF THE DEFENCE COMMITTEE OF THE KNESSET.
IT SAYS THERE THAT THERE ARE 111,000 POLICE AND SECURITY MEN MOBILIZED
TO GUARD THE SECURITY IN ISRAEL APART FROM THE ARMY. THIS IS THE MILITARY
MIRACLE IN THE SOUTH, INSOFAR AS IT IS A MIRACLE, I CAN TELL YOU HOW
SAD IT IS: THE RANGE OF OUR 23 MM. MACHINE-GUNS IS 3.5 KM. THE ISRAELI
AIRCRAFT FLY ABOVE THIS RANGE AND STRIKE OUR MACHINE-GUNS, ONE BY ONE,
BECAUSE OF THE INEQUALITY. ISN'T THIS AN INJUSTICE, COMRADE, THAT I
SHOULD STAND FACING THE MOST ADVANCED AMERICAN WEAPONRY WITH PRIMITIVE
WEAPONS, WHEREAS THE POLISARIO HAS THE MOST ADVANCED WEAPONS AND MISSILES
AGAINST THE SIMPLE MOROCCAN WEAPONS? WHAT DOES ALL THIS MEAN?
THE SIGNIFICANCE OF THIS IS THAT I FIGHT WITH MY BODY AND THE BODIES OF OUR
CHILDREN AND WOMEN, THIS IS THE PALESTINIAN MIRACLE.

PARALLEL TO THIS MILITARY STEADFASTNESS, WE HAVE MADE LARGE POLITICAL MOVES,
FOR EXAMPLE: OUR DELEGATIONS TO ASIA, AFRICA AND LATIN AMERICA ARE STILL
INTACT. WHEN NYRERE DECIDED TO TURN THE PLO OFFICE INTO AN EMBASSY, HE SAID
HE DISCOVERED THE ORGANIZATION AT HAVANA. WE RECEIVED 189 DELEGATIONS
DURING SIX MONTHS FROM ALL OVER THE WORLD.

GROMYKO: MOST OF WHOM WERE REPRESENTATIVES OF POPULAR ORGANIZATIONS?

ABU AMER: YES, ALL. I AM NOT SPEAKING ABOUT THE OFFICIAL DELEGATIONS. WE
MAINTAIN COORDINATION WITH THE AFRO-ASIAN SOLIDARITY COMMITTE, WITH THE
WORLD PEACE COUNCIL AND OTHER INTERNATIONAL INSTITUTIONS SUCH AS THE
DEMOCRATIC LAWYERS ASSOCIATION WHO, A WHILE AGO, HELD A SYMPOSIUM IN PARIS
AND CONDEMNED CAMP DAVID FROM THE JUDICIAL POINT OF VIEW. WE MADE DIPLOMATIC
MOVES IN THE COUNTRIES WE VISITED: VIENNA, ANKARA, MADRID, LISBON AND LATELY
THE MEETING I HAD WITH MARCHEE IN ORDER TO OBTAIN AN INVITATION FOR A VISIT
TO FRANCE. ALL THIS IN ADDITION TO OTHER ACTIVITIES, WHICH WE CONDUCT, AWARE
AS WE ARE OF THE FACT THAT SUCH ACTIVITIES HAVE AN INFLUENCE UP TO A CERTAIN
LIMIT AND THEREFORE WE HAVE NO ILLUSIONS ABOUT THEM.

WE HAVE REJECTED THE OLD IDEA WHICH STATES THAT WE SHOULD NOT BE IN THE SAME
PLACE WHERE THE ISRAELIS ARE   WE HAVE TO BE AHEAD OF THEM IN CONFERENCES, AS WAS
THE CASE IN THE CONFERENCE HELD BY THE ASSOCIATION OF LECTURERS OF
POLITICAL SCIENCE IN WHICH COMRADE PONOAMAREV PARTICIPATED, SINCE OUR
CASE IS STRONGER, AND THAT WAS WHAT HAPPENED IN THE ROME SYMPOSIUM TOO.

NOW LET US TALK ABOUT AN URGENT SUBJECT. WE FEAR WHAT MIGHT HAPPEN IN IRAN.
THE AMERICANS CONTACTED US THROUGH SOME ARAB STATES AND OTHERS AND OUR
ANSWER WAS CLEAR: WE ARE NOT INTERMEDIARIES , WE STAND BY THE IRANIAN
REVOLUTION.

GROMYKO: DID THE AMERICANS CONTACT YOU ON THEIR OWN INITIATIVE?

ABU AMER: NOT US (DIRECTLY BUT THROUGH) RAMSEY CLARK, WHO IS ONE OF OUR SYM-
PATHIZERS. WE DO NOT MEDIATE, WE SUPPORT THE IRANIAN REVOLUTION IN ITS JOY AND
IN ITS SORROW. KHOMEINI'S POSITION IS GOOD, AND HE SHOWS UNDERSTANDING TOWARDS
THIS POSITION OF OURS. WE SENT THE MANAGER OF THE MILITARY OPERATIONS ROOM
TO IRAN, SINCE THE MILITARY OPTION IS POSSIBLE ALTHOUGH IT IS WEAK
BUT IN ORDER TO BE SURE, I WOULD LIKE TO ASK MY COMRADES FOR
THEIR ESTIMATE, SINCE THEIR ESTIMATE IS MORE ACURATE THAN OURS. PRIOR TO
MY ARRIVAL HERE KHOMEINI CONTACTED ME AND ASKED FOR AN ASSESSMENT OF THE
SITUATION, BECAUSE WE OBSERVE THE PICTURE FROM THE OUTSIDE WHILE THEY SEE IT
FROM THE INSIDE. WE THINK SOMETHING MIGHT HAPPEN FROM THE DIRECTION OF AMMAN. I
TRIED TO BE AS BRIEF AS POSSIBLE, BUT WE MUST EXPECT AN ESCALATION IN LEBANON
AFTER OR DURING THE SUMMIT, IN ORDER TO ASSIST SARKIS   TO PRESENT
HIS VIEW. PRESSURE IS BEING PUT ON OUR PEOPLE IN THE OCCUPIED LAND SO THAT
THEY SHOULD AGREE TO AUTONOMY, FROM NOW UNTIL MAY 1980, WHEN THE MUNICIPAL
ELECTIONS WILL TAKE PLACE   WE INTEND TO DISCUSS OUR PROBLEM IN THE U.N. AND
WOULD LIKE TO HAVE YOUR SUPPORT FOR THE SUCCESS OF THE DECISION TAKEN IN
HAVANA. THIS IS A VERY IMPORTANT POINT.

THERE ARE RUMORS AMONG ISRAELI CIRCLES ABOUT INFLICTING A FATAL PREVENTIVE
ATTACK ON SYRIA. WE SAY THIS BECAUSE IN ISRAEL THERE ARE POLITICAL AND
ECONOMIC PROBLEMS WHICH THE ISRAELIS MAY TRY TO ESCAPE FROM BY EXPORTING
THEM OUTSIDE. THE POINT OF ORIGIN OF THIS ATTACK WILL BE LEBANON
SINCE IT IS CONSIDERED A WEAK POINT. THEY WILL(FIRST) ATTACK US
AND THE NATIONAL MOVEMENT AND LATER HIT SYRIA, INFLICTING A BLOW ON THE
SYRIAN FORCES IN LEBANON WOULD BE SIMPLE BECAUSE THEY ARE FULFILLING A
SECURITY MISSION AND NOT A MILITARY ONE.

PONOAMAREV: THERE ARE TWO QUESTIONS: YOU,COMRADE ARAFAT, WITH **THE** UNPRECEDENTED
RELATIONSHIP WITH AUSTRIA, AND YOUR MEETINGS WITH KREISKY AND BRANDT, DID YOU
PRESENT YOUR ASSESSMENT OF THESE ACHIEVEMENTS?

THE SECOND QUESTION CONCERNS THE SYRIAN TROOPS PRESENT ON LEBANESE TERRITORY:
DO THEY SUPPLY YOU WITH ARMS? DO THEY PARTICIPATE WITH YOU IN STOPPING THE
AGGRESSION?

ABU AMER: I WILL BEGIN WITH THE ANSWER TO THE SECOND QUESTION: THE SYRIAN
TROOPS ARE AT LATITUDE 37,10 AND THE FIGHTING, UNTIL NOW, TAKES PLACE SOUTH OF
THIS LINE. THEY ARE NOT PRESENT IN THE BATTLE AREA BETWEEN US AND THE ISRAELIS.
NEVERTHELESS THERE WERE TWO AIR CLASHES BETWEEN ISRAEL AND SYRIA. THE
SYRIANS ALSO DECIDED TO SEND SOME UNITS OF THE AIR DEFENSE IN ORDER TO
PROTECT THE (REFUGEE) CAMPS IN THEIR AREAS FROM ISRAELI AIR RAIDS. THIS,
ESPECIALLY AFTER ISRAEL ANNOUNCED IT WILL STRIKE AT THESE CAMPS, BECAUSE THE
FIGHTERS EXIT FROM THEM. WE SHOULD NOT OVERLOOK THE FACT THAT BOTH DAYAN AND
WEIZMAN ANNOUNCED THAT THIS WILL BE DONE IN COORDINATION WITH AMERICA, AND
THEREFORE THE IMPORTANCE OF THE POLITICAL DECISION OF SYRIA TO COUNTERACT.

AND AS REGARDS YOUR FIRST QUESTION RELATING TO THE **HORIZONS** OF POLITICAL ACTIVITY,
THE MATTER WHICH IS IMPORTANT TO US IN THIS CONTEXT IS TO EXPLAIN OUR
PROBLEM TO WORLD PUBLIC OPINION, AS, FOR EXAMPLE, TO THE NON-ALIGNED STATES.

I RECALL PARTICIPATING IN A CONFERENCE IN ALGERIA IN 1973 AND DESPITE THE
FACT THAT THE CONFERENCE TOOK PLACE IN ALGERIA WE DID NOT ACHIEVE THERE
WHAT WE ENDEAVOURED TO ACHIEVE. BUT OUR ACTIVITIES AMONG THE NON-ALIGNED
STATES DURING THE PAST SIX YEARS PRODUCED THE RESULTS AT HAVANA. OUR
ACTIVITY IN EUROPE IS BASED ON EUROPE'S NEED FOR ARAB OIL. OIL HAS NOT
YET BEEN INTRODUCED AS A FACTOR IN THE BATTLE, BUT THERE IS APPREHENSION
OF THAT THERE. SOME OF THE ARAB STATES HELP US IN THIS RESPECT.

PONOAMAREV: KREISKY BECAME A FRIEND OF THE ARABS?

ABU AMER: NOBODY SAYS SO. BUT WE HAVE TO PROFIT FROM IT.

PONOAMAREV: IT WAS AN ACHIEVEMENT AT LEAST THAT AFTER YOUR MEETING WITH HIM
(WITH KREISKY) CRACKS APEARED WITHIN THE ZIONIST CAMP. THIS BECAUSE HE WAS
PREVIOUSLY AMONG ISRAEL'S ADVOCATES.

GROMYKO: GOOD. THANK YOU FOR THE NEWS YOU BROUGHT ABOUT SOME OF THE
INTERNATIONAL PROBLEMS AND THE ASSESSMENT OF THE PRESENT SITUATION.

FIRST OF ALL I WILL SPEAK OF THE MAIN PROBLEMS OF INTERNATIONAL POLITICS,
AND ABOUT OUR POSITION CONCERNING THESE PROBLEMS, ALTHOUGH THIS POSITION IS
KNOWN AND I CAN DISCUSS IT IN BRIEF.

THE USSR CONTINUES ITS PRINCIPLED POLICY REGARDING THE MIDDLE EAST AS IT
DID IN THE PAST. WE ARE IN FAVOUR OF ISRAEL'S WITHDRAWAL FROM THE OCCUPIED
TERRITORIES AND IN FAVOUR OF GRANTING THE PALESTINIANS THEIR LEGITIMATE
RIGHTS AND THE ESTABLISHMENT OF THEIR INDEPENDENT STATE, TOGETHER WITH THE
RIGHT OF ALL THE STATES IN THE REGION TO BE SOVEREIGN STATES. THIS IS THE
ESSENCE OF OUR POSITION REGARDING THE MIDDLE EAST PROBLEMS.

WE FAVOUR A COMPREHENSIVE SETTLEMENT BUT ON CONDITION THAT IT BE A
JUST ONE. LEADERS IN THE ARAB WORLD (IN THE ORIGINAL TEXT THE WORD USED IS
'MESOULIN'' WHICH COULD ALSO BE TRANSLATED AS "RESPONSIBLE STATESMEN'')

CONCENTRATE ON A JUST SOLUTION AND WE SHARE THIS VIEW.

SADAT AND THE AMERICANS SPEAK OF A JUST SOLUTION BUT THEIR SOLUTION IS
UNJUST. NOW TOO, AS IN THE PAST, WE SHARPLY CONDEMN SEPARATE AGREEMENTS
WITH THE AGGRESSORS INCLUDING THE CAMP DAVID ACCORDS.

THE EXTERNAL FORM WHICH IS USED TO PRESENT THESE ACCORDS IS IRRELEVANT. THEIR
ESSENCE DID NOT CHANGE. THEY ARE ACCORDS OF TREASON FOR THE ARABS AND
THEIR INTERESTS. THE WHOLE WORLD KNOWS OUR POSITION AND OUR VIEW REGARDING
THE CAMP DAVID ACCORDS. IN OUR TALKS WITH THE AMERICANS WE DO NOT USE GENTLE
LANGUAGE. IN OUR MEETING WITH CARTER IN VIENNA, COMRADE BREZHNEV
PRESENTED THE STEADY SOVIET POSITION REGARDING THE VARIOUS PROBLEMS.
WE WANT OUR ARAB FRIENDS TO KNOW ABOUT THIS STEADY PRINCIPLED POSITION OF
OURS.

WE ATTACH SPECIAL IMPORTANCE TO THE PROBLEM OF UNITY IN THE ARAB WORLD. THE
MORE THE ARAB WORLD IS UNITED, THE MORE EGYPT'S SITUATION AND THE SITUATION
OF ITS LEADERSHIP DETERIORATE. WE IDENTIFY WITH YOUR VIEWS REGARDING THE TWO
BAGHDAD CONFERENCES. WE OBSERVED THE UNITY OF THE ARAB PEOPLES EXPRESSED IN
THESE TWO CONFERENCES WHERE IT WAS DECIDED TO TAKE A CORRECT POSTURE TOWARDS
THE POLICY OF THE IMPERIALISM AND ISRAEL AND THE EGYPTIAN LEADERSHIP. WE
WERE VERY SATISFIED WITH THE SUCCESS OF THE TWO CONFERENCES AND THE UNITY
OF THE ARAB PEOPLES ACHIEVED THERE. WE SINCERELY APPRECIATE - AND THIS IS
THE CLEAR-CUT OPINION OF THE SOVIET LEADERSHIP - THE ROLE OF THE PLO LEADERSHIP
AND THE ROLE YOU, COMRADE ARAFAT, PLAYED PERSONALLY IN THESE TWO CONFERENCES.

SOME OF THE PARTICIPANTS OF THE CONFERENCES WERE READY TO "BEND" TO THE
AGGRESSOR WERE IT NOT FOR THE ROLE YOU PLAYED. THERE WERE DIFFERENCES OF
OPINION IN THE CONFERENCE, BUT THE RESULT WAS FAVORABLE AND IT WAS
EXPRESSED IN THE SUCCESSFUL RESOLUTIONS.

THE SOVIET LEADERSHIP IS INTERESTED THAT THERE BE NO RETREAT FROM THE SUCCESSES AND ACHIEVEMENTS. THESE ACHIEVEMENTS MUST BE THE BASIS FOR THE NEXT ACTION. YOU CAN PLAY A ROLE IN THIS MATTER, YOUR ROLE WILL BE OF GREAT IMPORTANCE IN THE FUTURE.

WE ATTACHED IMPORTANCE TO MY CONVERSATION WITH KING HUSSEIN, THE MESSAGE OF WHICH WAS TO ADHERE TO THE NEED TO ESTABLISH AN INDEPENDENT STATE, IF THE PALESTINIANS SO WISH. WE NOTIFIED HADAM ABOUT THIS JORDANIAN POSITION AND HE SAID:"I RESPECT THIS DECLARATION BUT I HAVE MY DOUBTS REGARDING THE KING'S SINCERITY AND THE SERIOUSNESS OF HIS DECLARATION." IT SERVES OUR COMMON INTERESTS THAT THE KING SHOULD NOT RETREAT FROM HIS DECLARATION. YOU GAVE EMPHASIS TO THE IMPORTANCE OF THE COOPERATIVE ACTION BETWEEN YOU, SYRIA AND IRAQ IN THE STRUGGLE AGAINST CAMP DAVID, WE ATTRIBUTE TO THIS GREAT IMPORTANCE. YOU CAN PLAY A POSITIVE ROLE IN OVERCOMING THE DIFFERENCES BETWEEN SYRIA AND IRAQ , YOU HAVE NOT EXHAUSTED YOUR POSSIBILITIES IN THIS REGARD YET.

THERE IS ANOTHER MATTER WHICH YOU DID NOT MENTION BECAUSE OF LACK OF TIME, WHICH IS THE SAUDI ARABIAN POSITION IN THE LAST CONFERENCES - A POSITION WHICH WAS MUCH MORE POSITIVE THAN WE EXPECTED. POSSIBLY IT WAS INFLUENCED BY THE ATMOSPHERE EXISTING IN ALL THE CONFERENCES. THE OPINION OF THE SYRIANS IS THAT THERE ARE SEVERAL WEAK POINTS IN SAUDI ARABIAN POLICY EXPRESSED IN THE FEELINGS OF SOME MEMBERS OF THE ROYAL FAMILY, WHO THINK THAT THEIR DEFENSE AND SUPPORT CAN ONLY COME FROM THE AMERICANS.

IT SEEMS THAT THE "STEADFASTNESS FRONT" STATES HAVE ALREADY GAINED SOME EXPERIENCE IN HANDLING SAUDI ARABIA AND IN APPLYING PRESSURE ON IT.

ABU AMER: NOT ALL OF THEM.DEMOCRATIC YEMEN IS DIFFERENT IN THIS REGARD ESPECIALLY AFTER THE TREATY IT SIGNED WITH YOU.

GROMYKO: NOT DECISIVELY. THE IDEA IS THE INFLUENCE OF THE PLO AND OF
OTHER ARAB ELEMENTS. WE THINK YOU SHOULD EXPLOIT THIS EXPERIENCE,
BECAUSE OF THE IMPORTANCE OF THE SAUDI ARABIAN ROLE IN THE MIDDLE EAST
PROBLEM. AS FOR DEMOCRATIC YEMEN, ITS SITUATION IS DELICATE AND DIFFICULT.
BUT IT GOES ALONG WITH THE GENERAL STREAM IN THE POLICY OF THE "STEADFASTNESS
FRONT". SAUDI APPREHENSIONS OF OUR TREATY OF FRIENDSHIP WITH SOUTH
YEMEN HAVE NO BASIS, WE DO NOT INTERFERE WITH THE INTERNAL AFFAIRS OF
ANY COUNTRY. THE POSITION OF THE MOROCCAN KING IS NOT BASED ON PRINCIPLE
AND IS NOT EASY, WE SHOULD PREVENT THESE DIFFERENCES OF OPINION FROM
REMOVING KING HASSAN II FROM THE ARAB CONCENSUS.

YOUR EVALUATION OF THE ISRAELI-EGYPTIAN-AMERICAN STEPS CONCERNING THE
WEST BANK WAS CORRECT. WE ARE WITNESSING AN IMPERIALIST-ISRAELI-SADAT
CONSPIRACY. WE COULD UTTER SOME SHARP EXPRESSIONS ON THIS MATTER, BUT
THE IMPORTANT THING IS THAT WE AGREE WITH YOUR EVALUATION. YOU MENTIONED
THE AMERICAN COUNTER-ATTACK, THE ARABS ARE CAPABLE OF RESPONDING TO IT
IF THEY UNITE IN THE STRUGGLE AGAINST IT.

WHAT IS HAPPENING IN SOUTH LEBANON IS PART OF THE CONSPIRACY AND THE
SPEARHEAD OF THIS CONSPIRACY, AND IS DIRECTED AGAINST THE "PALESTINIAN RESISTANCE",
AGAINST SYRIA AND AGAINST LEBANON AS A SOVEREIGN STATE. WHEN WE ANALYZE
THIS SITUATION, WE DISCOVER THAT THE ALLIANCE BETWEEN SYRIA AND
THE "PALESTINIAN RESISTANCE" IN SOUTH LEBANON PLAYS A DECISIVE ROLE IN
THE STRUGGLE AGAINST THE AMERICAN ATTACK. YOU MENTIONED THE DIFFICULTIES
FACING YOU IN SOUTH LEBANON. DESPITE THE PHYSICAL DISTANCE BETWEEN US
WE APPRECIATE THE EXTENT OF THESE DIFFICULT PROBLEMS AND THE EFFORTS OF THE
"PALESTINIAN RESISTANCE" AND SYRIA TO CAUSE THE FAILURE OF THE AMERICAN
ATTACK.

AS FOR THE TUNIS CONFERENCE, THERE ARE DIFFERENCES OF OPINION REGARDING
THE SUCCESS OR FAILURE OF THIS CONFERENCE. THERE ARE REPORTS THAT SAUDI
ARABIA WILL PLAY A NOT-HONORABLE ROLE CONCERNING SOUTH LEBANON. BUT
THE FIVE "STEADFASTNESS FRONT" STATES CAN PLAY A ROLE IN BLOCKING THE
IMPERIALIST ASSAULT, BEARING IN MIND THAT SUCH A ROLE IS THE CORE FOR
NATIONAL ACTION, THE PURPOSE OF WHICH IS TO BRING ABOUT THE SUCCESS
OF THE SUMMIT.

THE WAY YOU DESCRIBED THE PROPOSALS OF PHILIP HABIB WAS TO THE POINT AND
ACCURATE. THESE ARE IMPERIALISTIC PROPOSALS AND ARE HOSTILE TO THE ARABS.
WE HOPE THE EVALUATION OF THE ARAB STATES WITH REGARD TO THESE PROPOSALS
WILL BE SIMILAR.

WE ALSO AGREE WITH YOU AS FAR AS THE INTERNATIONALIZATION OF THE LEBANESE
CRISIS IS CONCERNED. IF THIS DANGEROUS CONSPIRACY SUCCEEDS THEN IT WILL
PAVE THE WAY FOR AMERICA TO INFLUENCE HER FRIENDS IN EUROPE TO CAUSE THE
INTERNATIONALIZATION OF THE LEBANESE CRISIS. IT WILL HAVE A NEGATIVE
IMPACT ON THE ARAB INTERESTS AND, CONSEQUENTLY, IT WILL IMPROVE THE
ABILITY OF SADAT AND ISRAEL TO EXTEND THEIR INFLUENCE. I WISH TO
EMPHASIZE THE FACT THAT THE SOVIET POSITION REGARDING THESE CONSPIRACIES,
LIKE THE AUTONOMY CONSPIRACY AND THE CONSPIRACY TO INTERNATIONALIZE THE
LEBANESE CRISIS, WHICH PHILIP HABIB BROUGHT, IS NOT DIFFERENT FROM
THAT OF THE ARABS WHO ADHERE TO THEIR PRINCIPLES. FURTHERMORE, WE KNOW
THAT OUR SOCIALIST COMRADES SHARE THE SAME VIEW.

WE HEARD WITH SATISFACTION YOUR STATEMENT THAT 90% OF THE BAGHDAD RESO-
LUTIONS WERE IMPLEMENTED. THIS IS A SUCCESS FOR THE ARABS. IT IS THE FIRST
TIME I HEAR SUCH A CLEAR AND ACCURATE ASSESSMENT.

NOW I WISH TO MOVE ON TO SOME INTENATIONAL PROBLEMS.

IRAN: I REFER TO THE LAST EVENTS CONCERNING THE OCCUPATION OF THE AMERICAN
EMBASSY IN TEHERAN AND THE AMERICAN ACTIVITY CONNECTED WITH IT.

THE AMERICANS CONTACTED US A FEW DAYS AGO REQUESTING THAT WE PLAY A ROLE
IN THE AFFAIR THROUGH THE SENIOR FOREIGN DIPLOMAT IN TEHERAN, THE CZECH
AMBASSADOR, FOR THE PURPOSE OF FREEING THE AMERICAN DIPLOMATS.
WE INFORMED THE AMERICANS THAT WE ADHERE TO INTERNATIONAL AGREEMENTS AND
THAT OUR POSITION RESULTS FROM THE CONTENTS OF THESE AGREEMENTS (RELATING
TO DIPLOMATIC IMMUNITY).

IF WE LOOK AT THIS PROBLEM FROM THE POINT OF VIEW OF INTERNATIONAL AGREE-
MENTS, THEN WE MUST SHOW UNDERSTANDING TO THE AMERICANS AND THERE IS NO
JUSTIFICATION FOR IRAN TO CRITICISE US.

IF WE DON'T CONSIDER IT WITHIN THIS FRAMEWORK, BUT RATHER FROM THE POINT
OF VIEW OF AMERICAN–IRANIAN RELATIONS,THEN WE DO NOT WISH TO PROTECT
AMERICAN INTERESTS, DESPITE THEIR REQUEST THAT WE DO SO. THEREFORE, WE
WILL NOT GET INVOLVED IN A COMPLICATED DISCUSSION ON THE SUBJECT AND
IN NO WAY ARE WE GOING TO PROTECT THE AMERICANS IN THIS MATTER. WE
THINK THERE ARE NO DIFFERENCES OF OPINION BETWEEN US IN THIS MATTER,
DESPITE THE DIFFERENCE IN STATUS BETWEEN US - WE AS A STATE AND YOU
AS A NATIONAL LIBERATION MOVEMENT. THIS IS QUITE SATISFACTORY.

SO FAR WE HAVE NOT RECEIVED THE AMERICAN REACTION TO OUR RESPONSE.

ABU AMER: THE IRANIANS UNDERSTOOD FROM YOUR DELEGATE THAT HE ACCEPTED
THE AMERICAN REQUEST.

GROMYKO: OUR REPRESENTATIVE DID NOT OBJECT TO THE ANNOUNCEMENT OF THE
SECURITY COUNCIL CHAIRMAN,SINCE THIS IS A BRIEF DECLARATION CONCERNING
INTERNATIONAL AGREEMENTS REGARDING THE DIPLOMATIC CORPS.

ABU AMER: LET US NOT FORGET THAT THE DECLARATION INCLUDES SOME THREATS
OF USE OF FORCE.

GROMYKO: WE READ THIS DECLARATION AND FOUND IN IT NO MORE THAN THE FORMULATION
OF INTERNATIONAL AGREEMENTS REGARDING DIPLOMATIC REPRESENTATION, AND
THIS FORMULATION IS BALANCED. THERE WAS A SHARP DISPUTE ON THE SUBJECT
RELATING TO HINTS ABOUT USING FORCE. OUR POSITION, WHICH REJECTS
AND CONDEMNS SUCH ACTIONS, IS CLEAR.

WHEN THE IRANIAN REVOLUTION BROKE OUT, THERE WERE TALKS THEN ABOUT THE
USE OF FORCE. WE OPPOSED THIS LOGIC AND OUR POSITION REMAINS AS IT
WAS.

WE ARE NOW JUST PRIOR TO THE PRESENTATION OF THE PALESTINIAN ISSUE
IN THE U.N.,THIS MATTER IS VERY IMPORTANT TO US AND TO YOURSELVES.
THE QUESTION IS: WHAT DO YOU EXPECT FROM THE DISCUSSION? WHAT IS YOUR MINI-
MUM DEMAND OF THIS DISCUSSION? DID YOU THINK CAREFULLY ABOUT THE FORM IN
WHICH THE SUBJECT WILL BE PRESENTED AND HOW IT CAN BE ACHIEVED? I ASK YOU
TO ANSWER THIS AFTER I FINISH MY WORDS IN A SHORT WHILE.

WE WILL NO DOUBT SUPPORT AND ASSIST THE PALESTINIAN AND ARAB POSITION,
AND WE WILL BACK EVERY PROPOSAL AND EVERY PLAN WHICH YOU SUBMIT TO THE
U.N. THE SUPPORT FOR IT APPLIES TO OUR SOCIALIST COMRADES. THE LAST
QUESTION IS, AND IT IS ONLY A QUESTION: IT IS KNOWN THAT AMERICA - WHEN
IT TALKS WITH US ABOUT THE PALESTINIAN PROBLEM - ITS DELEGATES TELL
US: HOW IS IT POSSIBLE FOR US TO RECOGNIZE THE PLO AND THE ESTABLISHMENT
OF AN INDEPENDENT PALESTINIAN STATE WHEN THE PLO DOES NOT RECOGNIZE
ISRAEL AND THE WELL-KNOWN U.N. RESOLUTIONS. WE HEARD THE VERY
CONVINCING ARGUMENT FROM YOUR SIDE REGARDING THE MOTIVES
FOR YOUR REFUSAL TO ACCEPT THOSE (U.N.) RESOLUTIONS, SINCE THEY DEAL WITH
REFUGEES AND MAKE NO MENTION OF THE "PALESTINIAN PEOPLE". THESE REASONS
ARE KNOWN (TO US). BUT IN OUR TALKS WITH THE AMERICANS WE ALWAYS CONFRONT
THIS OBSTACLE AND THIS LIMITATION WHICH CANNOT BE OVERCOME.

HERE I WISH TO ASK YOU A QUESTION: ARE YOU CONSIDERING CERTAIN TACTICAL
CONCESSIONS IN RETURN FOR GETTING RECOGNITION FROM THE HOSTILE CAMP?
ARE YOU CONSIDERING RECOGNIZING THESE INTERNATIONAL RESOLUTIONS? AND ALSO
ARE YOU CONSIDERING RECOGNIZING ISRAEL'S RIGHT TO EXIST AS AN INDEPENDENT
SOVEREIGN STATE? I REMEMBER MY CONVERSATION WITH YIGAL ALLON WHO TOLD ME:
HOW CAN WE (ISRAEL) TALK WITH THE PLO WHEN THEY DO NOT RECOGNIZE ISRAEL'S RIGHT TO
EXIST AS AN INDEPENDENT STATE,AND WHEN THE PLO DOES NOT EVEN RECOGNIZE
THE U.N. RESOLUTIONS (CONCERNING THE ESTABLISHMENT OF THE STATE OF ISRAEL)?
HE ALSO TOLD ME THAT IF THE PLO RECOGNIZED ISRAEL AND THE U.N. RESOLUTIONS,
THE SITUATION WOULD BE DIFFERENT, AND IN THAT CASE WE (ISRAEL) WOULD HAVE
DEALT WITH IT IN A DIFFERENT MANNER.

MY QUESTION TO ALLON WAS: WHICH SIDE WILL MAKE THE FIRST STEP? THE PLO OR ISRAEL?
ALLON REPLIED:"IF ISRAEL WOULD HAVE INITIATED A DECLARATION IN THAT DIRECTION
(RECOGNITION OF THE PLO), THE PLO WOULD NOT HAVE AGREED TO ISSUE A SIMILAR
DECLARATION ON ITS BEHALF, BASED ON THE RECOGNITION OF ISRAEL AND THE U.N.
RESOLUTIONS." NOW THE GOVERNMENTS(IN ISRAEL)HAVE CHANGED, AND I DO NOT KNOW
WHAT YOUR (PLO) POSITION IS NOW.
I WOULD ALSO LIKE TO ASK YOU, IS YOUR POSITION THE REJECTION OF ALL NON-
PRINCIPLE CONCESSIONS RELATING TO THIS PROBLEM? WHAT MATTERS TO YOU IS THE
ESTABLISHMENT OF A PALESTINIAN STATE, AND, NOTWITHSTANDING THE DIFFERENCES
THAT MAY EXIST(AMONG YOURSELVES), THE ESTABLISHMENT OF A PALESTINIAN STATE
IS THE FOUNDATION AND CONTAINS ALL THE OTHER THINGS.

DURING THE DISCUSSIONS WITH THE AMERICANS WE FELT WE WERE IN
A DEAD-END. HERE I WOULD LIKE TO KNOW WHAT YOUR OPINION IS AND PLEASE
REGARD IT AS A QUESTION ONLY...

PONOAMAREV: YOU SPOKE ALONE, WHEREAS BOTH OF US SPOKE: GROMYKO PRESEN-
TED TO YOU IN DETAIL THE GENERAL DIRECTION OF THE SOVIET LEADERSHIP
TOWARDS THE MIDDLE EAST AND THE PALESTINIAN PROBLEM. WE KNOW, FROM
REPORTS WE HAVE RECEIVED AND FROM REPORTS YOU HAVE, THAT THE PLO
MARCHES ONWARD, AND YOU HAVE OUTGROWN THE FRAMEWORK OF AN ARAB LIBERA-
TION MOVEMENT. THE FACTS ARE KNOWN TO US AND THE RECOGNITION BY MANY
STATES IN THIS IS KNOWN. WE ARE VERY SATISFIED WITH THIS.

WE ASSISTED AND WILL CONTINUE TO ASSIST IN THE FUTURE (REFERRING TO
RECOGNITION).

WE THINK THAT THE GREETINGS COMRADE BREZHNEV CONVEYED TO YOU CONGRATU-
LATING YOU ON YOUR BIRTHDAY HELP THIS MATTER, AS DID THE MESSAGE COMRADE
BREZHNEV SENT TO BARCELONA. THIS WILL BE OF ASSISTANCE TO YOU FROM THE
ARAB AND INTERNATIONAL POINTS OF VIEW, TO ENABLE THE WORLD AND THE ARABS
TO UNDERSTAND THE PRINCIPLES OF SOVIET POLICY TOWARDS YOU.

BEFORE YOU ARE TWO MAJOR EVENTS:-

1.   THE TUNIS CONFERENCE.
2.   THE U.N. DEBATE ON THE (PALESTINIAN) PROBLEM.
YOU RAISED THE SUBJECT OF CONSULTATIONS ON THIS MATTER (OF THE U.N.
DEBATE). WE ALWAYS ASKED YOU TO CONSULT US ON THIS SUBJECT. IT IS VERY
IMPORTANT THAT WE KNOW IN ADVANCE THE STEPS OF THE ADVERSARIES IN THE
U.N. AND WILL KNOW HOW TO EXPLOIT THE U.N. STAGE BY EXPOSING AGGRES-
SIVE ACTIONS WHICH ISRAEL CONDUCTS IN SOUTH LEBANON. IT CAN NOT BE CON-
DEMNED INSIDE ISRAEL, BUT IN THE U.S. ISRAEL HAS FRIENDS AND THERE IS UTILITY
IN CAMPAIGNING TO EXPOSE ISRAEL'S ACTIONS AGAINST ELDERLY PEOPLE
AND CHILDREN, WHILE USING ALL MEANS OF PROPAGANDA.

AS REGARDS THE TUNIS CONFERENCE, YOU KNOW MORE THAN WE DO. WE AGREE
WITH YOUR OPINION THAT IT IS NOT WORTH DEVOTING THE WHOLE CONFERENCE
TO DISCUSSING THE SUBJECT OF SOUTH LEBANON AND TO AVOID A DEBATE ON THE
OVERALL PROBLEM, THE MIDDLE-EAST PROBLEM. IT IS VERY IMPORTANT THAT YOU
MOBILIZE ALL YOUR RESOURCES FOR THIS PURPOSE AND THAT YOUR ARAB FRIENDS
ARE ACTIVE SO THAT THE CONFERENCE WILL MAKE THE RIGHT DECISIONS

IT IS IMPORTANT THAT WE DEVOTE SPECIAL ATTENTION TO ALGERIA. LATELY WE
HAD STRONG TIES WITH ALGERIA. WE RECEIVED A PARTY DELEGATION (FROM
ALGERIA) AND SENT A COMRADE, BREZHNEV'S DEPUTY, TO PARTICIPATE IN THE
CEREMONIES IN ALGERIA. THEY TOLD US THAT PRESIDENT ALI SHADLI BEN JEDID
AND THE PARTY LEADER (OF THE REGIME) ZALLAH YECHIAWI, ARE DETERMINED TO
CONTINUE BOUMEDIENNE'S POLICY. THE SAME THINGS THE ALGERIANS TOLD OUR
DELEGATION CHIEF WHO ATTENDED THEIR CEREMONIES. ALGERIA'S WORD HAS
CONSIDERABLE WEIGHT NOW.

LATELY WE HAD CONTACTS WITH THE NATIONAL MOVEMENT IN LEBANON, ESPECIALLY
WITH THE COMMUNISTS AND JUMBALAT. ALL OF THEM STRESSED THAT THEIR RELATIONS
WITH THE PALESTINIANS ARE GOOD AND THAT THEY PARTICIPATE IN THE FIGHT
AGAINST THE ISRAELIS AND AGAINST THE REACTIONARY LEADERSHIPS IN THE
COUNTRY (LEBANON).

ABU AMER: THERE IS A JOINT COMMAND WHICH I HEAD.

PONOAMAREV: FOR THIS REASON IT IS VERY IMPORTANT THAT THE RELATIONSHIPS
BE GOOD, NOT ONLY WITH THE ANTI-IMPERIALIST ORGANIZATIONS IN LEBANON, BUT
ALSO WITH THE OTHER FORCES, LIKE FARANJIYE FOR INSTANCE. WE MUST HAVE
INFLUENCE ON THE LEADERSHIP OF THE LEBANESE STATE. IT IS NECESSARY THAT THE
SYRIANS PLAY A ROLE IN THE CONTACTS WITH LEBANON. OF COURSE, YOU, BECAUSE OF
YOUR PRESENCE IN LEBANON, MUST TAKE CARE THAT YOUR RELATIONS WITH THE LEBANESE
STATE (GOVERNMENT) SHOULD NOT WORSEN BECAUSE THEN YOUR SITUATION WOULD
BE DIFFICULT.

ABU AMER: OUR RELATIONS WITH AL HUS (LEBANON'S PRIME MINISTER) ARE GOOD,
WITH PRESIDENT SARKIS-NOT BAD. THE RELATIONS WITH THE ISLAMIC COUNCIL,
WITH THE NATIONAL FRONT AND WITH PRESIDENT FARANJIYE-GOOD. THIS YEAR WE
SPENT 19 MILLION LEBANESE POUNDS ON REPARATIONS FOR THE SOUTH AND NINE
MILLION POUNDS ON TREATING CIVILIANS.

PONOAMAREV: THIS IS YOUR MESSAGE AND IT IS GOOD. YOU HAVE TO PRESENT IT
IN THE U.N. AND IN TUNIS. TO END, I WOULD LIKE TO STRESS THAT IN ALL OUR
TALKS WITH THE ARABS, ESPECIALLY WITH PRESIDENT AL ASSAD, WE STATED (THE
NEED FOR) A JUST AND COMPREHENSIVE SOLUTION TO THE PALESTINIAN PROBLEM.
WE DECLARED THIS POSITION IN FORMAL TALKS, THROUGH THE PARTY AND

LATELY WE ESTABLISHED A COMMITTEE FOR FRIENDSHIP AND SOLIDARITY
WITH THE PALESTINIAN PEOPLE. WHEN THE VIETNAMESE PEOPLE STRUGGLED WITH THE
U.S.A. WE ESTABLISHED A SIMILAR COMMITTEE FOR SOLIDARITY WITH IT. VIETNAM, AS
WE KNOW, WON LATER, AND WE HOPE THAT THIS TIME VICTORY WILL BE ACHIEVED TOO.
THE COMMITTEE HAS BEEN ESTABLISHED AND WE WISH YOU EVERY SUCCESS.

ABU AMER: FOR OUR PART WE SET UP A COMMITTEE FOR SOLIDARITY WITH YOU. AS FOR
COMRADE GROMYKO'S QUESTION, WE ARE READY TO REPLY TO IT, IF IT WILL LEAD TO
ANY RESULTS, SINCE IT INDEED DESERVES AN EFFORT ON OUR PART.

KNOWING THAT WE ARE THE VICTIM, WE RAISED MANY POSSIBLE SOLUTIONS, WHILE
NONE OF OUR ENEMIES PRESENTED ANY. WE SAID: A DEMOCRATIC STATE WHERE JEWS
AND ARABS WILL LIVE. THEY (THE ISRAELIS) SAID: THIS MEANS THE DESTRUCTION
OF ISRAEL.

IN 1974 WE SAID WE WILL ESTABLISH THE PALESTINIAN STATE ON EVERY PART OF
LAND WHICH ISRAEL WITHDRAWS FROM OR WHICH WILL BE LIBERATED, AND THIS IS
OUR RIGHT. ARTICLE 1 IN THE PARTITION PLAN WHICH WAS IMPOSED ON OUR PEOPLE SAYS:
A PALESTINIAN STATE AND ISRAEL, THE RECONCILIATION COMMITTEE IN LAUSANNE
ADMITTED THE EXISTENCE OF TWO PROBLEMS: THE RETURN OF THE REFUGEES AND RECOG-
NITION OF A PALESTINIAN STATE. THEY (THE ISRAELIS) SAID: THIS(WILL BECOME)
A COMMUNIST STATE WHICH WILL STRIVE TO DESTROY ISRAEL. WHEN THE U.S.-SOVIET
JOINT COMMUNIQUE WAS PUBLISHED (REFERRING TO THE VANCE-GROMYKO STATEMENT IN
NEW YORK ON 1-2 OCTOBER 1977) WE ANNOUNCED THAT WE AGREED TO IT. WHAT DID
THE OTHERS OFFER? I CAN STAND IN FRONT OF THE U.N. AND ASK:WHAT DID THE
OTHERS PROPOSE? THEY SUGGESTED TO DEPART FROM THE PLO ("BYE BYE PLO"); A
MILITARY ATTACK (ON US) IN 1978- HELL DIRECTED AT US FROM THE SOUTH; THE
DESPICABLE CRIME CALLED "CAMP DAVID".

WE HAVE PROPOSED ALL THESE THINGS AND THEY HAVE OFFERED NOTHING. I SAY THAT
I AGREE TO THE SOVIET-AMERICAN COMMUNIQUE AND ACCEPT WHAT YOU AGREED
TO WITH THE AMERICANS.

GROMYKO: IN THE SOVIET-AMERICAN COMMUNIQUE THE GENEVA CONVENTION AND THE
PALESTINIAN RIGHTS ARE MENTIONED. THIS COMMUNIQUE WHICH YOU ASKED ABOUT, DID
NOT FIND EXPRESSION IN THE FIELD. IF IT WERE IMPLEMENTED, THE CIRCUMSTANCES
WOULD HAVE BEEN MORE FAVORABLE. I DO NOT WISH TO PUT PRESSURE ON YOU TO REPLY
TO THIS SUBJECT.

ABU AMER: THE PLO HAS NO DOUBTS.

GROMYKO: IF THERE IS ANY POINT IN PUBLISHING A JOINT COMMUNIQUE, WE HAVE A DRAFT WE ASK YOU TO LOOK AT.

Document II. Report on the Palestinian Delegation to the Soviet Union, January 22, 1981

The brother, head of the PLO Executive Committee, the General Commander of the Palestinian Revolutionary Forces, the brother Yasser Arafat, may Allah protect him.

Subject : Report on the Palestinian delegation to the Soviet Union

Date of report : 22 January 1981

On 1 September 1980, the delegation arrived in Simferopol (?) in the Soviet Union - the place decided on for holding the courses. The delegation numbered 194 officers and NCO's. Following are the types of courses:

1.   Tank battalion commanders

2.   Tank company commanders

3.   Infantry company commanders

4.   Reconnaissance company commanders

5.   Infantry platoon commanders

6.   Reconnaissance platoon commanders

7.   Anti-tank platoon commanders

8.   Sagger missile platoon commanders

9.   Anti-aircraft platoon commanders

Factions of the Resistance (movement) as follows :

1.   The Palestinian National Liberation Movement - Fatah

2.   The Palestinian Liberation Army

3.   The Armed Struggle

4.   The Popular Front

5.   The Democratic Front

NOTE: Original text in Arabic.

6.   The General Command

7.   Saiqa

8.   The Arab Front

9.   The Popular Struggle Front

10.   The Palestine Liberation Front

The studies at all the courses began in a regular fashion according to
the program which had been prepared. The delegation HQ studied the
program of each course and made comments which were taken into account
by the heads of the college and implemented in the study program as far
as possible, especially in connection with theoretical issues which suit
our conditions and actions in combat in towns, mountains, and in defence
of the coastal plain.

At the end of the study period in all the courses attended by the
delegation, the time arrived for the final manoeuvres, in which all
members of the delegation participated. The exercise included:

> a) HQ and staff exercise (work on maps).
>
> b) Tactical exercise

In the discussion during the exercise, the delegation HQ proposed that
the whole delegation carry out the HQ and staff exercise, in accordance
with the specialization of each course and its role in the battle, after
which a tactical exercise would be carried out. However, the HQ of the
college pointed out that the method which the delegation HQ wanted to
use was not possible, because it required many resources and the college
could not do this under those circumstances. In the end the delegation
HQ agreed with the opinion of the college and the exercise was carried
out in the following way:

> a) HQ and staff exercise at brigade level.
>
>> The battalion commanders course represented the brigade HQ
>> in the exercise. The brigade staff was made up of the various
>> courses. Altogether 17 officers participated. Work on the map
>> lasted for three consecutive days. The result was excellent -

according to the officers who supervised on behalf of the college. The work was done under the daily and personal supervision of the college commander. The HQ and staff exercise included the following stages:

(1) Advance in accordance with expectation of an encounter battle, "carrying out an encounter battle".

(2) Attack in direct contact.

(3) Defence.

b) On the fourth day of the exercise, the tactical exercise was begun by members of the delegation--an infantry company reinforced by a tank company in a direct contact attack. All types of organic and attached weapons were used in the exercise imitating a real battle. The exercise was carried out in earnest by the Palestinian combatant, despite the difficult weather conditions. The exercise was a success and earned the praise of the teachers, observers, and other delegations at the college.

Achievements of the delegation

1. In instruction

    a) Absorption of the study subjects in a good fashion. The teachers learnt that the Palestinian delegation is the best in absorbing quickly - unlike the other delegations.

    b) The anti-tank course teachers saw that the trainees prepared their guns and took up firing positions in less time than required.

    c) The teachers who accompanied the trainees on the anti-aircraft course on their trip into town (illegible) to the firing range saw that they were more than good.

d) The delegation showed good understanding during the discussion
of political subjects in the framework of the political
lessons, which the Soviet comrades deem very important and
concentrate on them.

2.   In the sphere of (the creation of) ties

a) Creation of good ties with the instructors and the workers
at the college.

b) Familiarisation with the customs and the tradition of the
peoples of the host country.

c) Explanation of the Palestinian cause and the role of the
PLO as the only legitimate representative of the Palestinian
people and the Palestinian revolution until the realization
of victory and the establishment of an independent state.

d) Getting to know the other delegations and liberation movements
and the establishment of good ties alongside the explanation
of our case, whether during personal meetings or in the framework of official meetings.

The commander of the delegation from South Africa showed full
understanding for our revolution and cause, so much so that during the
closing ceremony for his delegation he spoke in front of all the delegations and the Soviet comrades on the Palestinian revolution and Yasser
Arafat more than he spoke of himself and the host country.

Negative aspects on the subject of the delegation

1.   From the point of view of the college

a) Shortage of Arabic interpreters. At first the HQ of the
delegation had many difficulties concerning this matter.
Because of the constant request the college was compelled to
supply interpreters, but they did not succeed in rendering
exact military translations. In the end, in cooperation with

trainees of the other courses and with the new interpreters,
they overcame the problem, but not without great difficulty.

b) Shortage of clarification (illustration) means.

c) The training period for the anti-tank, missile and anti-
aircraft courses ended 15 days before the departure date,
forcing the college to repeat many of the lessons and
subjects.

d) Due to the size of the Palestinian delegation and the
presence of other delegations there, a third of the members
of the delegation had to sleep 10 to a room. This caused
difficulties, which were only overcome by a joint effort.

2. From the point of view of the delegation

a) The participants in the courses did not correctly understand
the political aspects of sending military delegations abroad.
As a result, the upper echelon of the delegation, namely the
participants in the battalion officers course, refused to study
and asked to return, using all sorts of illogical excuses. If
this is considered according to the correct military
criterion, and despite the possibility of overcoming these
difficulties very simply - if each one of them had remembered
the orders he received during his meeting with the commander of
the struggle. . . . before the trip - the situation would be
entirely different. This was written by the delegation HQ in
the report which was sent to Your Excellency through the
representative of the organization in Moscow, Amid Al Shaar,
on 22 September 1980.

b) Those responsible in most of the organisations were not care-
ful in choosing candidates for the courses, and this caused
the HQ of the delegation to return a small part. Following
are the names of the people returned, and the reasons for
their return:

First batch

(1) Raad Ahmed Razaq Al-Madani - from the PLA, was sent on
a reconnaissance company commanders course. He asked to
be transferred to the course for tank battalion
commanders. When the delegation HQ and PLO representative objected to this, he asked to return on the grounds
that there was no point in keeping him there.

(2) Haydar Jawad Safa - from the Democratic Front, tried to
create an organizational problem between the Democratic
Front and Popular Struggle Front, together with the
comrade Afif Al Masri of the Popular Struggle Front.

(3) Hassan Radha Bakr - from Saiqa, asked to return on the
grounds that his state of health did not allow him to
continue his studies. This was agreed upon in the
presence of the delegation HQ and a representative of
the organisation.

(4) Mohammad Radha Mahrar - from Saiqa, asked to return
because his state of health did not allow him to continue
his studies. This was agreed upon in the presence of the
delegation HQ, a representative of the organisation, and
the trainees' escort.

(5) Sahil Al Bitar - from the PLA, asked to return because
his state of health did not allow him to continue his
studies. This was agreed upon in the presence of the
delegation HQ and a representative of the organisation.

(6) Mulazzam Ibrahim Al Mahdoun - from the PLA, asked to
return because his state of health did not allow him to
continue his studies. When the Bulgarian "brother" came
there together with Raad Tamarzi, the commander of his
unit, he tried to persuade him (to stay) but to no
avail.

The second batch

(1) Ali Ahsan Al Najar - Palestine Liberation Front. Failed
in commanding the missile course and was a bad example
in military discipline because he used to jump from the
college wall, in contravention of the orders. The
delegation HQ also found out that he was connected with
the smuggling of counterfeit dollars.

(2) Afif Mohammad Al Masri - Struggle Front. He did not
behave himself outside the college. He spent his time
with one of the girls of doubtful character and accom-
panied her home. His clothes were later taken by a man
who claimed to the the girl's brother. He left her home
without his clothes and reported the incident to the
militia, which returned his clothes.

(3) Fawzi Al Asdi - Struggle Front. He spoke with the
representative of the organisation, (Al) Amid Al Shaar,
in an unbecoming manner. (Al-Shaar) asked that he be
returned. He was given another chance (and therefore)
was not sent back in the first batch.

When Aqid Abu Majdi came, the abovementioned asked to
immediately meet with him; following the meeting (I do
not know what went on there) Abu Majdi met with the
delegation HQ and comanders of the courses and mentioned
his name as one of those destined for return. When I
asked him why, he answered me that the above was a bad
man and he had to be returned. The comrade commander of
the college also informed me that he was one of those who
violated discipline by jumping from the wall of the
college.

(4) Darwish Dhib Saad - Arab Liberation Front. He is indecent
and a pervert. He got mixed up with a girl of doubtful
character. He claimed that she took his money together
with a report for the delegation HQ. The commander of
the delegation himself brought him from the city, drunk
as a lord.

(5) Ahmad Al Sharqi - Saiqa. He testified to the Simferopol (?)
inspector general (of the police?) during the investigation of the claim of one of the members of the delegation,
Hassan Qassem Hussein, that the militia and unidentified
people had beaten him and taken his money. In the course
of this evidence, Al Sharqi attacked by commander of
the college and threatened the college in the name of
the members of the delegation that if his friend's money
was not returned, "something would happen". Later on he
said to the inspector that when the Golan was captured,
Israel carried out body searches on the people but did
not take their money, while you - i.e. the Russians -
steal the people's money. This behaviour brought on a
serious response by the commander of the college and he
demanded that the man be returned, if possible.

(6) Salim Samir Asbar - PLA. Irregularities in training and
malingering despite the warnings given him.

(7) Mahmoud Nimr Shaqiqat - Fatah. Returned on his own
request. He incorrectly claimed that he had problems
with the Soviet comrades. We talked with him in order
to prevent his return, but he stuck to his position. It
was decided to grant his request in the presence of the
"brother" Abu Majdi, and his report to the delegation HQ
is attached herewith.

c) The problem of the counterfeit dollars

I have already given Your Excellency the report on this
problem through the organisation's representative in Moscow,
Amis Al Shaar, on 8 October 1980.

To His Honour the General Commander.

The return of the first and second batch has been completed in the hope
that this will deter those whose behaviour is bad, or those who were
mistakenly chosen. In spite of this, mistakes have been repeated. If the
delegation HQ needed again to return people and withhold certificates
according to orders, then half the delegation would have had to return.
However, in the interest of our revolution and our people the delegation
HQ invested all its efforts in absorbing as many as possible up to the
last moment, and this will be attested to by Aqid Abu Majdi himself, and
those who accompany him. For example, one of the members of the Popular
Front, whose name is Said Razaq(?), came back late from leave and arrived
at the college at 0430 in the morning. On the next day they celebrated
the end of the course, and the commander of the college decided to hold back
his certificate. We all agreed to this, including Abu Majdi. However,
after the certificates were distributed, the commander of the college
went back on his decision and gave the man his certificate.

Going by my experience in command of this large delegation, I ask your
permission, commander of the struggle, to put to you a number of simple
proposals and request that you study their usefulness, for the sake of
the good name of the revolution and our people in foreign countries.

Following are the proposals

1.   Opening of a training course for those who are to be sent abroad
before their departure (and in which they will study) the latest developments in the (Palestinian) problem and the aims - not connected with
studies - behind the dispatch of military delegations abroad.

2.   The holding of early checks by the instruction administration of
those intended to participate in courses as regard their suitability,
and the dispatch of only those who will pass the checks.

3.   The subordination of the officers to the course HQ so that their
personal ability as commanders can be checked without taking into
account the considerations of organisations or preferences according
to former opinions.

4.   Choice of people of high quality who are capable of representing
(us) outside, and the direct commander will bear the responsibility.

5.   Explanation to candidates for courses abroad with regard to
arrangements and rules in the absorbing college, before their trip.

6.   Lowering of the level of the courses abroad, sufficing with
courses for which there is no possibility for holding them in the
training directorate.

7.   If the need arises to send (to) courses of all types and
specialities; it is preferable to lower the number in order not to harm
the quality, and to allow a better selection.

8.   If a large number of courses are sent, it is advisable to appoint
a delegation commander who is not connected with any course and this will
be his only function. It is also advisable to use officers who have already
participated in a course at the same college, and who know its rules.

9.   The military delegations in foreign countries must have a large
number of books in foreign languages, especially in the language of the
host country - in political, historical and cultural subjects. They
should also have PLO stickers and slogans in booklets and publications,
etc.

10.   Similar material should also be sent by post.

Sir, the supreme commander, may God protect him, I am sending this report
on behalf of the PLO delegation in the Soviet Union and pledge our
adherence to wise behaviour which will guide us to the victory and

the establishment of our independent state. Long live the PLO under
your leadership, the sole legal representative of the Palestinian
people.

Signed : Muqadam Rashad Ahmed, commander of the delegation.

Document III. Graduation Certificate of the Ministry of Defense, USSR

МИНИСТЕРСТВО ОБОРОНЫ СССР

СВИДЕТЕЛЬСТВО

АН № 13661

Настоящее свидетельство выдано ......
РААФАТУ АБД ЭР-РАХМАНУ
АХМАДУ СИЛЬМИ
в том, что он .... в СЕНТЯБРЕ 1980 г. поступил ....
и в ЯНВАРЕ 1981 г. окончил ....
ОФИЦЕРСКИЕ КУРСЫ

по специальности ....КОМАНДИР
РАЗВЕДЫВАТЕЛЬНОГО ВЗВОДА

Настоящее свидетельство дает право на
самостоятельное выполнение работ, связан-
ных с полученной специальностью.

Начальник

"20" ЯНВАРЯ 1981 г.

М. П.

Регистрационный №

THE MINISTRY OF DEFENCE, USSR

CERTIFICATE

AN № 13661

This is to certify that أفنت عبد الرحمن أحمد سلمي

دخل ما طلقا هذه الشهادة في الملك عام؟

entered in ١٩٨٠ 19 and graduated

from , في كانون الثاني ١٩٨١ ك

من دورة الضباط لبسة قائد فصيلة

استطلاع 19

majoring in ....

The bearer of the Present Certificate enjoys
the privilege for independent activity associated
with the Major Subject.

Commanding Officer

"١٩٨١/١/٢٠" 19

S. P.

Registration No.

Graduation certificate of the Ministry of Defense, USSR, awarded to Rafat 'Abd-al-Rahman Ahmad Silmi. He completed a course for platoon commanders (reconnaissance) in January 1981.

Document IV. Graduation Certificate of the Ministry of Defense, USSR

МИНИСТЕРСТВО ОБОРОНЫ СССР

СВИДЕТЕЛЬСТВО

АН № 13765

Настоящее свидетельство выдано
капитану
Абдул-Азизу Махмуду Абу-Феддалу
в том, что он ч окт. 1975 поступил
: ч марта 1976 окончил *I Высшие*
Офицерские курсы „Выстрел"

по специальности: *командир пе-*
хотного батальона

Настоящее свидетельство дает право на
самостоятельное выполнение работ, связан-
ных с получением специальностью.

Начальник I курсов „Выстрел"
генерал полковник вид
(Д. драгунский)
26 марта 1976

Регистрационный 3012/146

THE MINISTRY OF DEFENCE, USSR

CERTIFICATE

AN № 13765

This is to certify that *Captain*
Abdul-Aziz Mahmood Abu-Feddal

entered in *October* 19 75 and graduated
from *the Vystrel Academy*

in *March* 19 76
majoring in *the course of Infant-*
ry Battalion Commander

The bearer of the Present Certificate enjoys
the privilege for independent activity associated
with the Major Subject.

Commanding Officer Vystrel Academy
colonel general of a record corps
(D. dragunsky)
26 *March* 19 76
Registration No. 3012/146

Graduation certificate of the Ministry of Defense, USSR, awarded to
Captain Abdul-Aziz Mahmood Abu-Feddal. He completed a course for
infantry battalion commanders in March 1976.

Document V. Graduation Certificate of the Ministry of Defense, USSR

МИНИСТЕРСТВО ОБОРОНЫ СССР	THE MINISTRY OF DEFENCE, USSR
СВИДЕТЕ___ЬСТВО	**CERTIFICATE**
АН № 19441	АН № 19441
Настоящее свидетельство выдано *Тагер Хасан Хуссейн*	This is to certify that *Taher Hassan Hussein*
в том, что он в *мае* 1976 г. поступил и в *ноябре* 1976. окончил *офицерские курсы*	entered in *May* 1976 and grad...ted from *the officers' course* in *November* 1976
по специальности *командира артиллерийско - мино-менной батареи*	majoring in *the speciality of the artillery and mortar battery commander*
Настоящее свидетельство дает право на самостоятельное выполнение работ, связанных с полученной специальностью.	The bearer of the Present Certificate enjoys the privilege for independent activity associated with the Major Subject.
Начальник	Commanding Officer
м. п. *11 - ноября* 1976 г. Регистрационный № *394*	S. P. *11 - November* 1976 Registration No. *394*

Graduation certificate of the Ministry of Defense, USSR, awarded by a Soviet army officer to Taher Hassan Hussein, who completed a course for artillery and mortar commanders on November 11, 1976.

Document VI. Graduation Certificate of the Hungarian Military Academy

Igazolvány száma

MOHAMED FARLIN
KADOR

(rendfokozat)

Harckocsivezető

T-34

jogosult ....

.... gyártmányú és típusú
harckocsikat, rohamlövegeket vezetni.

(Hk. vez. sajátkezű aláírása)

(Pk. aláírása)

196./.. év ..febr.. hó 26 napján.

541. rsz. P. H.
MNHF — 69.38622 Közl. Ny. — 340

.... sz. alakulat 198./...év
..febr.. hó 26 napján kelt...../...számú
parancsa alapján
III. Osztályú harckocsivezető-vé
lépett elő.
Az előléptetés időpontjában...............................

T-34 .... gyártmányú

harckocsin 12 ....üzemóra vezetői
gyakorlattal rendelkezik.
Technikai felkészültségének foka. ....

....

....

(az előléptetést elrendelő pk. aláírása)
196.1... év febr. hó 26. napján.
P. H.

Graduation certificate of the Hungarian Military Academy awarded to
Mohamed Farlin Kador. He completed a course for T-34 tank drivers
in February 1981.

Document VII. Graduation Certificate of Vietnam

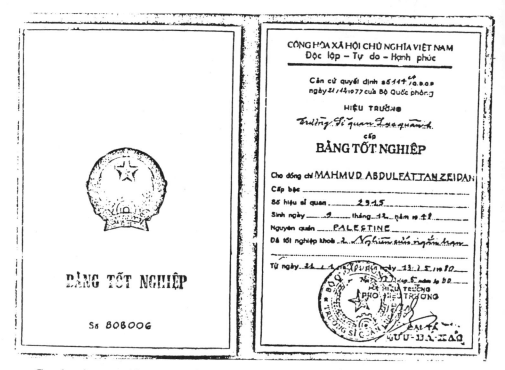

Graduation certificate of Vietnam awarded to Mahmud Abdul-Fattan Zeidan (born in "Palestine"). He completed a course in May 1980.

Document VIII. An "RPG Kid"

An "RPG kid," typical of several hundred children (ages 10–15) trained by the PLO to operate Soviet-made rocket-propelled grenades.

Document IX. PLO Members and Foreign Guerrillas Studying a Model of a Soviet Tank

In a course at a Soviet training base, PLO members and foreign guerrillas study a model of a Soviet tank.

Document X. Courses Officers and NCOs Took in Foreign Countries

SUBJECT: List of Courses which officers and NCOs of the "September-Martyrs-Battalion"/Castel
Brigade/Fatah took in foreign countries
Source: Handwritten list captured in Sidon
(Remark: The original list includes courses taken in Arab countries.)

No.	Military ID No.	Rank	Name	Date present rank received	Course, Date, Place
1.	31487	Major	Faisal Muhamed Alsheich Yusef	--	1. Military Academy, China; 2. Battalion Commanders Course, Moscow; 2. Staff Officers, Pakistan, 1979.
2.	44552	Capt.	Jamal Yakov Jadan	Feb. 1, 1976	1. Fadayin Commander, Moscow; 2. Armor, Hungary, 1980.
3.	41054	1st Lt.	Fchal Muhamed Otman	1975	1. Platoon Commander, Moscow, 1975-6; 2. Company Commander, Vietnam, 1977-8.
4.	44818	1st Lt.	Muhamed Abd Allah Slamah	Jan. 1, 1976	1. Company Commander, China, 1977; 2. Armor Company Commanders, Moscow.
5.	32242	1st Lt.	Juad Ahmed 'Abdul-Ghani	Jan. 1, 1976	1. Political training, China, 1978-9; 2. Political training, Bulgaria, 1979-80.
6.	31492	2d Lt.	Rateb Nussa Mahmud Abu-Samarah	1975	1. Infantry Company Commander, Moscow, 1977; 2. Armor, Hungary, 1979.
7.	31281	2d Lt.	Yassin Hatchar Muhamed	Sept. 1, 1976	1. Armor, Hungary, 1980; 2. Armor Company Commander, Moscow.
8.	13644	2d Lt.	Ahmed Mustafa Hamdan Ghana'im	June 1, 1977	1. Armor Company Commander, Pakistan, J.T.A., 1978.

Note: A selection of entries; original text in Arabic.

No.	Military ID No.	Rank	Name	Date present rank received	Course, Date, Place
9.	51009	2d Lt.	Ibrahim Shachda 'Amar	June 1, 1977	1. Armor Company Commander, Pakistan, 1978; 2. Armor Communication, Pakistan, 1979.
10.	74709	2d Lt.	Said Ibrahim al-Ghazzi	June 1, 1977	1. Armor Company Commander, Pakistan, 1978; 2. Armor, Hungary, 1979.
11.	46897	2d Lt.	Khaled Issa Abd Hassan	June 1, 1977	1. Armor (Preparatory Course), Pakistan, 1979; 2. Armor, Hungary, 1980; 3. Armor Company Commander, Pakistan.
12.	52524	2d Lt.	Hassin Muhamed Ahmed Said	April 27, 1978	Armor, Hungary, 1979.
13.	13463	2d Lt.	Zaki Muhamed Ibrahim Alsheich	April 27, 1978	Armor, Hungary, 1979.
14.	15361	2d Lt.	Mustafa Hassan Mustafa Kandeil	April 27, 1978	1. Social Studies, Bulgaria, 1979; 2. Armor, Hungary, 1980.
15.	31708	2d Lt.	Ahmed Hassin Ahmed Ja'Aber	April 27, 1978	Armor, Hungary
16.	15372	2d Lt.	Ibrahim Raja Zalah Alhamzat	April 27, 1978	Armor, Hungary
17.	73937	2d Lt.	Ahmed Muhamed Ahmed Mari Alsharkawi	April 27, 1978	A/A Company Commander, Moscow.
18.	22029	2d Lt.	Ahmed Fazal Muhamed Abu Halil	April 27, 1978	Armor, Hungary
19.	21008	Serg. Major	Sha'ar Mustafa Ibrahim Mustafa	Mar. 1, 1977	1. Armor Platoons, Pakistan, 1978; 2. Armor, Hungary, 1980.
20.	53477	Serg. Major	Abd Alrahman Ahmed Hassin Alsharif	April 6, 1977	1. Armor, Hungary, 1980; 2. Military Academy, Cuba, 1979.

Document XI. Sports Stadium in Beirut

This sports stadium in Beirut was used by the PLO as a training and arsenal center.

Document XII. Fatah Poster

This Fatah poster vows that the battle against the Jewish state (symbolized by the Star of David) will continue in the path of Zeheir Muhsin, assassinated PLO leader.

Document XIII. Relations of Palestinian Terrorist Groups with the "Front for the Liberation of the Central Arab Desert"

"POPULAR FRONT FOR THE LIBERATION OF PALESTINE"

GENERAL COMMAND

MILITARY H/Q

With the discovery of the plan a battle broke out on 15 May, 200 soldiers were killed and 3 officers from the Niger forces succeeded to arrest "Nakib" Sidi Muhamed, 2 officers and the soldiers that carried out the coup. But the "Imam" who is the Secretary-General of the "Front" succeeded in escaping through the desert to Mauritania. There, he and his deputy, Muhamed Mussa, met with Polisario fighters and reached Libya, where they stayed.

The secret activity of the revolution, deep in Mali territory, continued. The revolution organized a widespread underground movement by recruiting masses of people, ideologically guiding them, and by the establishment of a monetary fund. This in order to enable the payment of 10 million Francs for the release of the leader, Ziad Ben Taher, who found refuge in Algeria. Ben Bella extradited him to the Mali Government which jailed him in 1963 and did not free him until 1979, now he is in Mali under supervision. The revolution continued secret recruiting, every recruit had to swear by the Koran that he will be loyal to the revolution and will never reveal any of its secrets.

The founding conference of the "Front" took place in 1979 with the participation of all its leaders. There the organizational skeleton of the "Front" was laid out, the camps and offices were opened in Libya in coordination with Algeria.

The goals of the "Front for the Liberation of the Central Arab Desert" are:

1. The liberation of the Central Arab Desert from the colonialism of Mali and Niger and reuniting it.

2. Annexation of the Desert to the Arab homeland and uniting it with any Arab country wishing to do so.

3. Turning Arabic into the official language of the Desert.

4. The establishment of a free, democratic state, its slogan being:"Freedom, Islamic Socialism and Unity".

5. War with colonialism, imperialism, Zionism amd racial discrimination.

6. Liberation of the "Desert" citizen from all binds.

7. The liberation of the national economy from foreign control.

8. Removal of the foreign bases located in the north.

Translator's comment:
There is no date on the original Arab document.

Document XIV. Excerpts from the Report of the International Department of the PFLP for June 1980

LIBERATION MOVEMENT DEPARTMENT

DURING THE CURRENT YEAR THE DEPARTMENT CARRIED OUT THE FOLLOWING ACTIVITY:

A. WITH THE ARGENTINIAN WORKERS PARTY:
THE DEPARTMENT HOSTED AN ARGENTIANIAN DELEGATION FOR A PERIOD OF SIX MONTHS. A COMPREHENSIVE PROGRAM WAS PREPARED FOR THEM AND JOINT MEETINGS AND COURSES WERE HELD TO FAMILIARIZE THEM WITH THE STRUGGLE OF THE PALESTINIAN AND ARGENTINIAN PEOPLES.

B. WITH THE REVOLUTIONARY FRONT FOR THE RESTORATION OF EAST TIMOR'S INDEPENDENCE:
ON INVITATION OF THE PALESTINE LIBERATION ORGANIZATION, A DELEGATION AND THE MAN IN CHARGE OF INTERNATIONAL RELATIONS OF THE FRONT ARRIVED IN BEIRUT. THE FRONT MET WITH THE ABOVE MEMBER AND THE PROBLEMS OF PALESTINE AND EAST TIMOR WERE REVIEWED. HE TOURED SEVERAL INSTITUTIONS OF THE FRONT.

C. WITH THE POPULAR FRONT FOR THE LIBERATION OF ERITREA:
A MEETING WAS HELD WITH THEM IN WHICH THE VIEWS AND POSITIONS OF BOTH SIDES WERE PRESENTED. IN THE MEETINGS DISCUSSIONS TOOK PLACE ON THE VISIT OF MANGISTO TO SUDAN AND THE NEGATIVE AFFECT THIS HAS ON THE REBELLION IN ERITREA.

Document XV. Activity for the Liberation Movement Department of the PFLP in July 1980

ACTIVITY OF THE LIBERATION MOVEMENT DEPARTMENT OF THE
PFLP IN JULY 1980

A. A MEETING WAS HELD WITH A DELEGATION COMPRISING MEMBERS
   OF THE CHILEAN COMMUNIST PARTY AND THE WORKERS AND FARMERS
   (LENINIST AND MARXIST) PARTY IN CHILE. THEY VISITED
   LEBANON ON THE INVITATION PRESENTED TO THEM BY THE
   POPULAR FRONT FOR THE LIBERATION OF PALESTINE. THEY
   VISITED LEBANON FOR A WHOLE WEEK DURING WHICH THEY BECAME
   ACQUAINTED AT FIRST HAND WITH THE MILITARY ACTIVITY
   OF THE FRONT AND ALSO WITH THE INFORMATION AND COMMUNAL
   ACTIVITY OF THE FRONT. POLITICAL MEETINGS WERE HELD IN
   WHICH THE POLITICAL SITUATION IN SOUTH AMERICA AND THE ARAB
   WORLD WERE DISCUSSED. THE MEETING ENDED WITH THE SIGNING
   OF AN AGREEMENT OF COOPERATION WITH THE TWO PARTIES.
B. LETTERS WERE SENT TO THE IRANIAN FREEDOM FIGHTERS IN
   ORDER TO FAMILIARIZE THEM WITH THE POLITICAL SITUATION
   IN THE ARAB REGION AND IN ORDER TO STRENGTHEN THE TIES.
C. A TELEGRAM OF GREETINGS WAS SENT FOLLOWING THE FOUNDING
   OF THE ETHIOPIAN WORKERS PARTY.
D. A LETTER WAS SENT TO THE ETHIOPIANS IN WHICH IT WAS
   REQUESTED TO STRENGTHEN THE TIES WITH THEM.
E. A LETTER WAS SENT TO AFGHANISTAN IN WHICH WE RENEWED
   THE INVITATION FOR A VISIT.

Document XVI. The "European Base" at Shatila, 1981

1. THE "EUROPEAN BASE" IS LOCATED IN THE SHATILA REFUGEE CAMP (BEIRUT).
   THE COMMANDER OF THE BASE IS AREF KHATEB, HIS CODENAMES ARE "ABU EL
   ABED" AND "MASRASA EL KAHAL". HIS DEPUTY IS NAKIB (CAPTAIN) HASSAN
   MAZ'AL.

2. THE BASE SERVES AS A PLACE OF INSTRUCTION AND TRAINING FOR VARIOUS
   TERRORIST GROUPS SUCH AS THE "RED BERETS"*, "BADER MEINHOFF",
   "TURKISH LIBERATION ARMY", INDIANS, PAKISTANIS AND IRISHMEN.

3. THE DURATION OF A COURSE IS 45 DAYS, DURING WHICH THE TERRORISTS
   STUDY DEMOLITION MATERIALS, SMALL ARMS OPERATION, KARATE AND MILITARY
   TACTICS.

4. THE TRAINING WEEK WAS FROM MONDAY TO SATURDAY AFTERNOON.

5. THE FOLLOWING IS THE LIST OF INSTRUCTORS KNOWN TO THE CAPTURED TERRORIST:

   A. MULAZEM AWAL (LIEUTENANT) NAMER HAJAJ: INTERPRETER.
   B. MULAZEM AWAL (LIEUTENANT) SAID BAHIT: INTERPRETER.
   C. MULAZEM AWAL (LIEUTENANT) ABU VAGDI: WEAPONS INSTRUCTOR.
   D. NAKIB (CAPTAIN) ISMAIL YASIN: KARATE INSTRUCTOR.
   E. NAKIB (CAPTAIN) ADNAN HASEIKI: DEMOLITION MATERIALS INSTRUCTOR.
   F. MULAZEM (2ND LIEUTENANT) ABU EL FATOUAH: DEMOLITION MATERIALS INSTRUCTOR.
   G. MULAZEM (2ND LIEUTENANT) IBRAHIM A-GANDAN: MILITARY TACTICS INSTRUCTOR.
   H. MULAZEM (2ND LIEUTENANT) ANWAR ABU IBRAHIM: MILITARY TACTICS INSTRUCTOR.
   I. MUKADAM (MAJOR) TAISIR EL HASSAN: INTELLIGENCE AND BASE SECURITY
      OFFICER; THIS OFFICER GIVES POLITICAL LECTURES AND IS IN CHARGE OF
      IDENTIFYING FOREIGN INTELLIGENCE AGENTS.

*PROBABLY THE "RED BRIGADES".

6. THERE IS NO SINGLE BRANCH IN THE FATAH WHICH IS IN CHARGE OF FOREIGN TERRORISTS GROUPS. THE FOLLOWING IS A LIST OF ORGANS OF THE FATAH, EACH OF WHICH IS FINANCIALLY RESPONSIBLE FOR ANY FOREIGN GROUP BROUGHT TO THE EUROPEAN BASE UNDER ITS AUSPICES:

   A. INTELLIGENCE APPARATUS - COMMANDER,"ABU A ZA'IM".
   B. CENTRAL SECURITY APPARATUS - COMMANDER,"ABU EL-HUL".
   C. JOINT SECURITY APPARATUS - COMMANDER "ABU IYAD".
   D. WESTERN SECTOR SECURITY APPARATUS - COMMANDER, HALIL EL-WAZIR ("ABU JIHAD"

7. IN AUGUST 1981 46 GERMANS ARRIVED AT THE BASE. ALL TERRORISTS PRESENT AT THE BASE AT THE TIME WERE TRANSFERRED TO THE "BIR HASSAN" BASE.

8. IN NOVEMBER 1981 FIVE BRITONS, THREE WOMEN AND TWO MEN, ARRIVED AT THE BASE; THEY WERE MEMBERS OF A BRITISH COMMUNIST PARTY DELEGATION HEADED BY THE SECRETARY OF THE PARTY.

Document XVII. Excerpts from the Report on the Discussions of the Palestinian Military Mission to East Germany, April 14 to 19, 1982

The mission arrived at the East Berlin airport at 13:00 and was received by the East German deputy defense minister, the Chief of Staff and several senior officers. The Deputy Defense Minister presented our itinerary to us:

Day 1, April 14: No official discussions.

Day 2, April 15: Discussions on the subject of training with the officer in charge of recruitment and training at the military academies.

A colonel from the assistant defense minister's office will visit you in the afternoon. He will present the final draft of the military assistance agreement detailing the assistance which we plan to provide and he will decide the delivery timetable with you. This will enable us to prepare a final draft agreement for signature.

Day 3, April 16: A visit to an infantry recruitment and training camp so that you may observe the facilities and training program, the firing ranges, the naval facilities, grenade throwing instruction and anti-aircraft procedures. All of these things can help you. Consultations with air and naval defense experts will follow.

Day 4, April 17: Discussion with our export agency and a tour of the city.

Day 5, April 18: A tour of Berlin.

Day 6, April 19: The signing of the agreement followed by an official dinner and a special tour of the city. Departure for Hungary.

NOTE: Original text in Arabic.

Record of Events

Thursday, April 15: Military training discussions.

East German senior officer: As a result of the discussions held last October between the assistant defense minister and the deputy commander of the P.L.O., we agreed to assign P.L.O. trainees to our military academies and to train them. I want to tell you, comrades, that our officer training program consists of the following components:

1. Political indoctrination: An introduction to sociology and political science as a background to the purpose of military training. A military officer is directly responsible for this area.
2. Technical and tactical training.
3. Physical training.
4. There are also courses in Math, Physics and the German language.

The Marxist-Leninist doctrine serves as the basis for all training. Do you have any objection to this?

Reply: Absolutely not!

Question from the P.L.O. delegation: Will the P.L.O. trainees be segregated? We prefer that they be trained alongside German trainees.

Answer: While we do not have a special camp for the Palestinians, they will be a separate group. This is because of their limited knowledge of German and because German officers also learn Russian.

The P.L.O. delegation reiterates its request that P.L.O. trainees learn alongside German trainees, if possible.

East German senior officer: There are additional problems. As I already explained to the deputy commander of the P.L.O., our training period is three years. Our artillery course is comprehensive and we train for speed. Your deputy Commander requested that we shorten the training time and we agreed up to the battery level.

Question: A question was asked by the delegation concerning the number of trainees and the level they will reach.

Answer: In our previous discussions (with the deputy Commander) the number of trainees was agreed upon and that they would be taught to use Soviet weapons.

Question: The delegation requests to increase the number of trainees and to strengthen the P.L.O. ties with the (East) German army as well as with the German people.

Answer: Basically, no changes will be made in the number of trainees or in the training program. We will send you a detailed schedule via the embassy and, if the number of trainees can be increased, we will notify you and attach an addendum to the agreement.

Question: Can there be changes in the specializations in respect to those agreed upon?

Answer: Modifications in the training plan will incur additional expenses. Requests to learn additional skills should be referred to the Soviet Union.

Question: If the additions are approved, we should like 10 people from the armoured and 10 people from the Engineering.

Answer: We agree and will notify you via the embassy before the 30th of May.

The agreement was presented for review and approved.

The delegation expressed its appreciation for the understanding and interest in our needs and wish to convey an invitation to the Minister of Defense from the Deputy Commander of the P.L.O. to visit us. (The Deputy Defense Minister suggested that the Minister be invited when he stops over at the airport. He also wished to notify the Deputy Commander that the Minister of Defense will visit Damascus in September and would like to meet him and the P.L.O. Commander there.)

The delegation requested to meet with the Minister of Defense to personally invite him to send regards from the P.L.O. Commander and his deputy.

Thursday Afternoon

Several officers from the Ministry of Defense.
—Welcomed us and informed us that they are empowered by the Deputy Defense Minister to discuss military aid with us.
—Apologized that the Minister of Defense was unable to meet with us.
The delegation expressed its understanding.

Acquisitions 18.4.82, 10:00 hours

The export manager had a list of the purchase prices of the items we requested.

1. Small patrol craft with only rocket armament: $118,000.
2. 14.5 MM ammunition.
     Anti-tank bullets, type B-32, at a price of $1,608.— per 22,500 shells.
     Anti-tank bullets, type BZT, at a price of $1,792.— per 22,500.
     Standard bullets, at $2,498.— per 45,000.
3. Shilka artillery pieces, 6 pieces at $1,587.— million each.
4. Ammunition for 27 MM artillery pieces
     —$6.— per anti-aircraft shell in quantities of 51,000.
     —$7.— per anti-tank shell in quantities of 122.
5. Ammunition for 57 MM artillery pieces
     —$29.— per anti-tank shell in quantities of 12,000.
     —$33.— per anti-tank shell in quantities of 12,000.
6. Ammunition for 100 MM artillery pieces
     —$70.— per anti-tank shell in quantities of 2,000.
7. 122 MM gun shells
     A. $160.— per shell for up to 1,100 explosive shells.
     B. $100.— per shell for up to   250 illumination shells.
     C. $140.— per shell for up to   280 training shells.

8. 130 MM field pieces
   a. Each at a cost of $92,000.—for up to 10 pieces.
   b. *Ammunition*
      1) Full load: $344.3   for up to 1,520 shells.
      2) Incomplete load: $251.— for up to 1,800 shells.
      3) Anti-tank: $379.5 for up to   270 shells.
9. Military compasses—$5.— each.

Delivery Schedule

Part of the order can be received immediately and part within four weeks of establishment of a credit line in the bank.

The prices are F.O.B. Rostok Port of the Democratic Republic of Germany.

—There will be a 10% surcharge if delivery is to Torlus Port.

—A discount of 2% applied to the total bill.

Note—Price lists and catalogues are available from Brother 'Akid' Abu Chaled.

Monday 11:00 o'clock

The Protocol and its attachments were signed in the presence of the Deputy Defense Minister. This was followed by an official dinner and the presentation of gifts.

Monday 19:00 o'clock

A dinner was held at the home of the Palestinean Ambassador attended by the Deputy Minister of Defense and all the others who participated in the discussions.

The Deputy Minister of Defense made a speech expressing his astonishment at the courtesy and abilities of the delegation and its high military, professional and political level.

Notes

Chapter 1. Terrorism: The Strategic Dimension

1. H. R. Simpson, "Terror," *U.S. Naval Academy Proceedings* 96 (1970): 64–69.

2. John Collins, "Definitional Aspects," in *Political Terrorism and Energy: The Threat and Response,* ed. Yonah Alexander and Charles Ebinger (New York: Praeger Publishers, 1982), p. 11.

3. Ray S. Cline, "Foreword," in *Behavioral and Quantitative Perspective on Terrorism,* ed. Yonah Alexander and John Gleason (Elmsford, N.Y.: Pergamon Press, 1981).

4. For some details on assistance given to terrorists by various governments in recent years, see, e.g., *Congressional Record,* vol. 123, May 9, 1977, S-7253.

Chapter 2. Soviet Ideologies and Policies

1. Unpublished remarks by Senator Jeremiah Denton (Republican from Alabama), Chairman of the Subcommittee on Security and Terrorism, Committee on the Judiciary, U.S. Senate, February 2, 1983.

2. Karl Marx, *Das Kapital* (Berlin: Dietz Verlag, 1962), p. 779.

3. Arnold Kunzli and Karl Marx, *Eine Psychographie* (Wien, Frankfurt, Zurich: Europe Verlag, 1966), pp. 703, 712, 715.

4. Marx, *Das Kapital,* p. 779.

5. V. I. Lenin, "Partisan Warfare," in *Modern Guerrilla Warfare,* ed. F. M. Osanka (New York: Free Press of Glencoe, 1966), p. 68. See also V. I. Lenin, "Left-Wing Communism—and Infantile Disorder," in *Selected Works* (Moscow: Progress Publishers, 1975), 3:301.

6. Ibid.

7. R. Ulyanovsky, "Present-day Problems in Asia and Africa," in *Theory, Politics, Personalities* (Moscow: Progress Publishers, 1980), p. 36.

8. Leon Trotsky, Preface to *Terrorism and Communism* (Ann Arbor: University of Michigan Press, 1961), pp. xix–xxxvi. This volume was also published under the titles *The Defence of Terrorism* and *Dictatorship vs. Democracy.*

9. For these and other Soviet doctrinal pronouncements, see Foy D. Kohler, et al., *Soviet Strategy for the Seventies,* Miami University unpublished monograph, 1973.

10. *TASS,* January 22, 1961.

11. *New York Times,* January 18, 1961.

12. U.S. Congress, Senate, Committee on the Judiciary, Subcommittee on Security and Terrorism, *Historical Antecedents of Soviet Terrorism, Hearings,* 97th Cong. 1st sess., June 11–12, 1981.

13. Great Britain, Foreign Office, Document 371/8170, N. 476 (1922).

14. Ibid., N. 9302 (June 22, 1922).

15. Ibid., October 12, 1922.

16. Ibid., File 123, 1922.

17. Ibid., Documents 371/10478 (June 16, 1924) and 371/10841 (December 18, 1924, and January 5, 1925).

18. *Times* (London), May 26, 1927.

19. Great Britain, Foreign Office, Documents 371/15600, N. 3024, and N. 3686/1970/38 (1931) and 371/15592, N. 3435/4/48, N. 3440/4/38, N. 3793/4/38 (1931) and 141/532 (1935).

20. Ibid., Document 371/15213, c. 1740 (March 19, 1931).

21. See, e.g., Hugh Thomas, *The Spanish Civil War,* 3d ed. (Harmondsworth: Penguin Books, 1979), pp. 120–123.

22. Great Britain, Foreign Office, Document 371/15072 (1931).

23. Ibid., Document 371/20342, N. 5360 (1936).

24. Ibid. N. 47/47/38 (1936).

25. Lord Chalfont, "Freedom in Danger: The External and Internal Threat," *Atlantic Community Quarterly,* Fall 1976.

26. See, e.g., I. Brownlie, *International Law and the Use of Force by States* (New York: Oxford University Press, 1963), pp. 241–242.

27. "The Treaty of Peace Between Lithuania and the Soviet Union," signed on July 12, 1920, *British and Foreign State Papers,* vol. 113, p. 1121; *Soviet Documents on Foreign Policy,* ed. J. Degras (London: Oxford University Press, 1951), 1:296, for the protocol of the Riga Conference, March 30, 1922, to which Estonia, Latvia, Poland, and the Soviet Russia were parties; Ian Brownlie, "International Law and the Activities of Armed Bands," *International and Comparative Law Quarterly* 7 (1958): 720–721, for other agreements to which the Soviet Union has been a party in the years 1920–1932; J. Stone, *Aggression and World Order* (Berkeley: University of California Press, 1958), for Soviet attitudes on the question of terrorism.

28. Yonah Alexander, Marjorie Ann Browne, and Allan S. Nanes, eds., *Control of Terrorism: International Documents* (New York: Crane, Russak, 1979); Robert A. Friedlander, *Terrorism: Documents of International and Local Control* (Dobbs Ferry, N.Y.: Oceana Publications, 1979).

29. United Nations, General Assembly, 27th Session, U.N. Document A/C 6/SR 1389 (December 13, 1972), pp. 4–5.

30. Ibid. U.N. Document A/AC 160/1, Addendum 1, June 12, 1973, Ad Hoc Committee on International Terrorism, July 16–August 10, 1973, p. 26.

31. See, e.g., Ray S. Cline, *Soviet Policy in a Global Perspective: Implications for Western Policy* (Washington, D.C.: Center for Strategic and International Studies, Georgetown University, March 25, 1975).

32. *Annual of Power and Conflict, 1973–1974* (London: Institute for the Study of Conflict, 1974), pp. 230–258.

33. Y. V. Andropov, *Speeches and Writings* (New York: Pergamon Press, 1983), p. 5.

34. Ibid., p. 31.

Chapter 3: Charges and Countercharges

1. Remarks made by Ambassador Edward Marks, Coordinator for Anti-Terrorism Programs, U.S. Department of State, at a news conference sponsored by the Institute for Studies in International Terrorism, State University of New York, New York City, February 15, 1983.

2. *New York Times,* June 26, 1979, and January 15, 1981.

3. Ibid., January 28, 1981.

4. Ibid., January 29, 1981.

5. *Christian Science Monitor,* January 30, 1981; *Washington Post,* February 7, 1981; and "Terrorism: Russia's Secret Weapon?" *U.S. News and World Report,* May 4, 1981, p. 27.

6. *Washington Post* and *New York Times,* April 28, 1981.

7. *Strategic Review* 1 (Spring 1981): 9.

8. *TASS,* July 21, 1982.

9. Ibid., February 7, 1981.

10. *Pravda,* June 20, 1981.

11. *Moscow Domestic Service,* July 17, 1981.

12. *Izvestia,* July 15, 1981.

13. *Moscow Domestic Service* (Russian), July 17, 1981.

14. *TASS,* July 21, 1981; *Radio Moscow* (Polish), July 20, 1981; *Radio Moscow* to North America, July 21, 1981; *Pravda,* September 6, 1981.

15. *Izvestia,* July 14, 1981. A book review entitled *International Terrorism and the CIA* by Brosi Sveto and Oleg Tarin appeared in *TASS* on February 2, 1981. It enumerated CIA activities, including alleged assassination plans of the past two decades.

16. *TASS,* January 15, 1982.
17. *Pravda,* July 8, 1981.
18. *TASS,* July 16, 1981.
19. Ibid., August 18, 1981; *Radio Moscow* (Persian), July 9, 1981.
20. *Moscow International Service,* July 10, 1981.
21. *Moscow Domestic Service,* July 17, 1981.
22. *Moscow World Service,* June 30, 1981; *Radio Moscow* (Greek), June 14, 1981; *TASS,* February 1, 1981.
23. *Radio Moscow,* January 26, 1982.
24. *TASS,* September 11, 1981. According to this report a U.S. *Special Services Document,* FM-30-31, was discovered among the possessions of the daughter of a Fascist head of a Masonic Lodge. "This document said directly that it was necessary to use terrorist movements in friendly countries in the interests of the United States." *TASS* "presumed" that the CIA was also behind the Red Brigades kidnapping/murder of the Italian Christian Democratic leader Aldo Moro because he advocated cooperation with Italy's Communist Party. On September 4, 1981, *Radio Moscow* stated that the CIA supports the activities of the "fascist terrorist groups to whom the Pope's assailant Turk Mehmet Ali Agca belongs, as well as that of leftist gangs such as the Red Brigades in Italy." On January 21, 1982, *Radio Moscow* claimed that General Dozier was kidnapped by Red Brigades in order for NATO to justify further strengthening of control in Italy.
25. *Sovetskaya Kultura,* September 15, 1982.
26. *Baku International Service* (Azeri), July 12, 1981, citing *Tehran Times* report.
27. *TASS,* February 8, 1982.
28. Ibid., July 17 and 21, 1981.
29. *Radio Moscow* (Persian), June 29, 1981.
30. *Pravda,* July 19, 1981.
31. *Izvestia,* June 30 and July 18, 1981; *Moscow Domestic Service,* July 23, 1981.
32. *Moscow Domestic Service,* July 15, 1981; *Izvestia,* June 30, 1981; *Moscow World Service,* June 30, 1981; *TASS,* September 14 and 30, 1981.
33. *TASS,* July 21, 1981.
34. *Radio Moscow,* September 4, 1981.
35. *TASS,* December 24, 1982.
36. *Bloody Traces of American Imperialism:* Soviet title to this collection is *Krovavyi Sledy Amerikanskogo Imperdrializma* (Moscow: Mysl' Publisher, 1982). The book has not yet been translated.

37. V. M. Sergeev, *Secret War Against Cuba* (Moscow: Progress Publishers, 1982).

38. A. Aseevskii. *Who Organizes and Directs International Terrorism?* (Moscow: Political Literature, 1982).

39. See, e.g., Associated Press, December 8, 1982.

40. *New York Times,* December 9 and 10, 1982.

41. Ibid., December 23, 1982.

42. Ibid., September 23, 1982.

43. *Christian Science Monitor,* January 30, 1981; *Washington Post,* February 7, 1981; *New York Times,* February 9 and May 31, 1981; and Blaine Harden, "Terrorism," *Washington Post Magazine,* March 15, 1981.

44. U.S. Congress, Senate, Committee on the Judiciary, Subcommittee on Security and Terrorism, *Hearings,* 97th Cong., 1st sess., April 24, 1981.

45. Unpublished remarks provided by Senator Jeremiah Denton's staff, Subcommittee on Security and Terrorism.

Chapter 4. The PLO Transmission Belt

1. *The PLO, the Soviet Union, and International Terrorism,* (Jerusalem: Israel Information Center, August 30, 1981).

2. For an excellent survey, see Y. Harkabi, *Fedayeen Action and Arab Strategy* (London: Institute for Strategic Studies, December 1968).

3. See Fouad M. Moughrabi, "The Palestine Resistance Movement: Evolution of a Strategy." Paper delivered at the 17th Annual Convention of the International Studies Association, Toronto, Canada, February 25–29, 1976.

4. For a description of the organizational development of the Palestinian movements together with an examination of the political ideologies of the various groups, see, e.g., Leila S. Kadi, *Basic Political Documents of the Armed Palestinian Resistance Movement* (Beirut: Fifth of June Society, n.d.). This report, by Gerard Chaliand, was originally published in *Le Monde Diplomatique,* March 1969. For a more recent study, see Aaron David Miller, *The PLO and the Politics of Survival* (New York: Praeger Publishers, 1983) (Washington Papers/99, vol. 11 of the Center for Strategic and International Studies, Georgetown University, Washington, D.C.).

5. Oriana Fallaci's interview with George Habash in *Life,* June 12, 1970.

6. Robert Kilmarx and Yonah Alexander, eds., *Business and the Middle East: Threats and Prospects* (Elmsford, N.Y.: Pergamon Press, 1982).

7. Ibid.

8. *ADL Special Report,* Summer 1981, p. 33. For information on other meetings, see *Syrian News Agency,* July 10, 1977; and Yonah Alexander, "Some Soviet-PLO Linkages," *Middle East Review* 14 (Spring–Summer 1982): 65.

9. Interview with *Radio Monte Carlo,* February 17, 1981.

10. See Document I, Appendix, p. 83.

11. Quoted in *ADL Special Report,* Summer 1981, p. 30.

12. *New York Times,* November 29, 1980.

13. Ibid., February 24, 1981; see also Alexander, "Some Soviet-PLO Linkages."

14. *TASS,* October 20, 1981.

15. Ibid.

16. Ibid.

17. *New York Times,* September 15, 1982.

18. Quoted by *Algiers Domestic Service* in French, February 15, 1983.

19. Quoted by *Algiers Voice of Palestine* in Arabic, February 16, 1983.

20. *KUNA* in English, September 15, 1982.

21. *TASS* in English, September 19, 1982.

22. Ibid., September 21, 1982.

23. *Voice of Palestine,* April 27, 1979.

24. *Literaturnaya Gazetta* as reported by *TASS,* October 21, 1981.

25. *Voice of Palestine,* January 27, 1982.

26. Ibid., October 26, 1980.

27. Ibid., October 21, 1981.

28. Interview with *Al-Dustur* (London), April 30, 1979.

29. Interview with *Al-Watan Al-Arabi* (Paris), May 4, 1979.

30. Interview with *Monday Morning* (Beirut), November 22, 1981.

31. Quoted by *Reuters* (Beirut), April 8, 1980.

32. "Foreign Report," *The Economist,* May 19, 1983.

33. *Al Ahram,* July 11, 1978.

34. "Foreign Report," *The Economist,* May 16, 1979.

35. Interview with *Al Medina* (Saudi Arabia), November 13, 1979.

36. Quoted by *Radio Monte Carlo,* January 8, 1980.

37. Quoted by *Reuters,* January 8, 1980.

38. An interview with *Monday Morning* (Beirut), January 18, 1981.

39. An interview with *Al-Rai Al-Aam* (Kuwait), August 17, 1981.

40. *Al-Qabas,* March 9, 1981, and *AFL* (weekly), November 28, 1980.

41. *WAFA* and *Novosti* reports of December 1980.

42. *Ath-Thawra,* January 13, 1981, and *Voice of Palestine,* June 21, 1981.

43. "International and Transnational Terrorism," *The Central Intelligence Agency,* April 1976; *Daily Telegraph,* April 3, 1979.

44. *Daily Telegraph,* September 5, 1979.

45. *ADL Special Report,* Summer 1981.

46. *New York Times,* November 2, 1980.

47. Israeli media reports, 1981.

48. Ibid.

49. CIA Report, April 1976. See also U.S. Congress, Senate, Foreign Relations Committee, *Hearings on International Terrorism,* September 19, 1977.

50. "Foreign Report," *The Economist,* June 14, 1978; *L'Express* (Paris), January 13, 1981.

51. Quoted in *ADL Special Report,* Summer 1981.

52. *Radio Monte Carlo,* February 17, 1981.

53. Interview with *Al-Liwa* (Lebanon), August 6, 1979.

54. Israeli media reports.

55. *New York Times,* October 31, 1980, and *Information Digest,* June 23, 1982, p. 221.

56. Documents personally obtained through intelligence sources in Lebanon and Israel during several trips in the summer of 1982, December 1982–January 1983, March–April 1983, and July–August 1983.

57. *Daily Telegraph* (London), July 16, 1979. See also *New York Times,* April 25, 1979. Israel television also reported details on September 23, 1980.

58. *Al-Watan Al-Arabi,* July 17, 1978; *Al Ahali* (Cairo), July 28, 1978.

59. *A-Sharq Al-Awsat* (London), September 13, 1979.

60. *Life,* June 12, 1970, pp. 33–34.

61. U.S. Congress, Senate, Committee on the Judiciary, *Hearings on Terrorist Activities,* May 14, 1975; *Life,* June 12, 1970.

62. *An-Nahar* (Beirut), January 21, 1977.

63. *Al-Said* (Lebanon), July 28, 1977.

64. *An-Nahar* (Beirut), January 21, 1978.

65. *Al-Qabas* (Lebanon), August 27, 1978.

66. Various Israeli media reports.

67. *Al-Hawadath* (London), January 27, 1979.
68. According to Free Lebanon Forces Commander Major Sa'ad Haddad, August 21, 1979.
69. *Associated Press,* reporting from Lebanon, May 5, 1980.
70. *Sunday Times* (Holland), March 2, 1980.
71. *Al-Amal* (Lebanon), December 31, 1980.
72. *Al-Liwa,* February 8, 1981.
73. *Akhbar al Osboua* (Jordan), August 12, 1981.
74. *PLO Radio,* October 27, 1981.
75. *Al-Huwadeth* (Beirut), November 6, 1981.
76. Ibid., November 12, 1981.
77. *PLO Radio,* November 15 and 17, 1981; *East German News Agency,* November 17, 1981.
78. *Monday Morning* (Beirut), December 6, 1981.
79. *L'Express,* December 9, 1981.
80. Personal interviews.
81. Information provided by the Israeli Defense Forces spokesman, October 21, 1982.
82. Reported by *Jerusalem Domestic Service,* February 9, 1983.
83. *Kuwaiti al-Majallah,* June 18, 1983.
84. Y. V. Andropov, *Speeches and Writings* (New York: Pergamon Press, 1983), pp. 233–234.

Chapter 5. International Infrastructure of Terrorism

1. *Pravda,* September 29, 1964.
2. "International and Transnational Terrorism," CIA, April 1976. According to this report, "the Soviet Union carries on a program of bringing youth revolutionaries from all parts of the Third World to the Soviet Union for training and indoctrination" (p. 20).
3. *Le Point,* June 21, 1976.
4. John Barron, *KGB: The Secret Work of Soviet Secret Agents* (New York: Bantam Books, 1974), pp. 76–77; Christopher Dobson and Ronald Payne, *The Terrorists: Their Weapons, Leaders, and Tactics* (New York: Facts on File, 1979).
5. *Congressional Record,* September 15, 1978, p. E-5036.
6. Cited by Aydin Yalcin, "Terrorism in Turkey," June 25, 1981, p. 1 (unpublished paper).
7. Brian Crozier, "The Direct Support." Paper delivered at the Jerusalem Conference on International Terrorism, sponsored by the Jonathan Institute, July 2–5, 1979.

8. *Christian Science Monitor,* March 14, 1977, pp. 14–15.

9. "International and Transnational Terrorism," CIA, April 1976, p. 20.

10. Dobson and Payne, *The Terrorists.*

11. *The Economist,* January 1, 1977, p. 50.

12. *Washington Post,* September 7, 1975, p. B5.

13. Vittorfranco S. Pisano, *Contemporary Italian Terrorism: Analysis and Countermeasures* (Washington, D.C.: Law Library, Library of Congress, 1979).

14. *New York Times,* March 23, 1983

15. Walter Laqueur, *Terrorism* (Boston: Little, Brown & Co., 1977), pp. 200–201.

16. U.S. Congress, Senate, Committee on the Judiciary, *Hearings,* May 14, 1975, part 4, p. 194.

17. Institute for the Study of Conflict, *Conflict Studies,* no. 69 (1976): 9–10.

18. Ibid.

19. *Christian Science Monitor,* March 15, 1977, pp. 14–15.

20. *Far Eastern Economic Review,* October 14, 1977, p. 16.

21. Senator Denton's unpublished remarks, February 2, 1983, p. 7.

22. Ibid.

23. *Daily Telegraph* (London), June 6, 1980.

24. Risk International, "Executive Risk Assessment," October 1982.

25. "Foreign Report," *The Economist,* February 14, 1980.

26. See Yonah Alexander, "Terror International: The PLO-IRA Connection," *American Professors for Peace in the Middle East Bulletin,* October 1979, p. 3.

27. Yonah Alexander, "International Network of Terrorism," *Political Terrorism and Business,* ed. Yonah Alexander and Robert A. Kilmarx (New York: Praeger Publishers, 1979), pp. 50–51.

28. *PLO Radio,* January 12, 1982.

29. *Ath-Thawra,* May 2, 1981.

30. Briefing (Israeli Foreign Ministry), May 16, 1982, p. 4.

31. *Elseviers Magazine* (Amsterdam), September 1, 1979.

32. *New York Times,* May 26, 1977, p. 8; June 4, 1977, p. 8.

33. *Foreign Broadcast Information Service,* June 5, 1978.

34. *Congressional Record,* April 26, 1978, p. S-6426.

35. "Foreign Report," *The Economist,* March 24, 1983.

36. *Defense and Foreign Affairs Weekly* 14 (April 4–10, 1983): pp. 4–5.

37. *Foreign Broadcast Information Service,* February 1, 1979.
38. CIA, April 1976.
39. *New York Times,* July 16, 1976, pp. 1, 6.
40. *Foreign Broadcast Information Service,* March 24, 1978.
41. *New York Times,* July 16, 1976, pp. 1, 6.
42. *Foreign Broadcast Information Service,* January 18, 1978.
43. *Christian Science Monitor,* March 14, 1977, p. 31.
44. *New York Times,* June 12, 1972, p. 1.
45. *Washington Post,* May 13, 1977, p. A23.
46. *Al-Anwar* (Lebanon), May 22, 1976.
47. *Congressional Record,* May 26, 1978, p. S-6426.
48. Based on informal briefing by U.S. Department of State, May 25, 1983.
49. Ibid.
50. *Time,* October 24, 1977.
51. *Christian Science Monitor,* March 15, 1977, pp. 14–15.
52. *Miami Herald,* July 7, 1978.
53. *Los Angeles Times,* March 19, 1976.
54. *New York Times,* October 9, 1977.
55. *Miami Herald,* July 7, 1978.
56. *London Times,* October 18, 1977.
57. Ibid.
58. *Wall Street Journal,* April 15, 1980.
59. State Department, May 25, 1983.
60. Ibid.
61. Ibid.
62. Ibid.
63. Unpublished paper by Senator Denton's staff, p. 3.

Chapter 6. The United States Confronts Wars of Liberation

1. Y. V. Andropov, *Speeches and Writings* (New York: Pergamon Press, 1983), pp. 82, 83.
2. Ibid., pp. 249, 250.

Bibliography

Adeniran, Tunde, and Alexander, Yonah, eds. *International Violence.* New York: Praeger Publishers, 1983.

Afanasyev, V. G. *Marxist Philosophy.* Moscow: Progress, 1978.

Alexander, Yonah, ed. *International Terrorism: National, Regional, and Global Perspectives.* New York: Praeger Publishers, 1976.

Alexander, Yonah; Browne, Marjorie Ann; and Nanes, Allan S., eds. *Control of Terrorism: International Documents.* New York: Crane, Russak, 1979.

Alexander, Yonah; Carlton, David; and Wilkinson, Paul, eds. *Terrorism: Theory and Practice.* Boulder, Colo.: Westview Press, 1979.

Alexander, Yonah, and Ebinger, Charles K., eds. *Political Terrorism and Energy: The Threat and Response.* New York: Praeger Publishers, 1982.

Alexander, Yonah, and Friedlander, Robert A., eds. *Self-Determination: National, Regional, and Global Perspectives.* Boulder, Colo.: Westview Press, 1979.

Alexander, Yonah, and Gleason, John M., eds. *Behavioral and Quantative Perspectives on Terrorism.* Elmsford, N.Y.: Pergamon Press, 1981.

Alexander, Yonah, and Kilmarx, Robert A., eds. *Political Terrorism and Business: The Threat and Response.* New York: Praeger Publishers, 1982.

Alexander, Yonah, and Seymour, M. Finger, eds. *Terrorism: Interdisciplinary Perspectives.* New York: John Jay Press, 1977; New York: McGraw-Hill Book Co., 1978.

Ali, Tariq, ed. *The New Revolutionaries: A Handbook of the International Radical Left.* New York: William Morrow & Co., 1969.

Arendt, Hannah. *The Origins of Totalitarianism.* New York: World Publishing Co., 1963.

Avrich, Paul. *The Russian Anarchists.* Princeton: Princeton University Press, 1967.

Bassiouni, M. Cherif, ed. *International Terrorism and Political Crimes.* Springfield, Ill.: Charles C. Thomas, 1975.

Baumann, Carol Edler. *The Diplomatic Kidnappings.* The Hague: Nijhoff, 1973.

Bell, J. Bowyer. *A Time of Terror: How Democratic Societies Respond to Revolutionary Violence.* New York: Basic Books, 1978.

————. *Transnational Terror*. Washington, D.C.: American Enterprise Institute for Public Policy Research, 1975.

Beres, Louis René. *Terrorism and Global Security: The Nuclear Threat*. Boulder, Colo.: Westview Press, 1979.

Bernardo, Teixeira. *The Fabric of Terror*. New York: Devin-Adair Co., 1965.

Brinton, Crane. *The Anatomy of Revolution*. New York: Vantage Books, 1960.

Burton, Anthony M. *Revolutionary Violence: The Theories*. New York: Crane, Russak, 1978.

————. *Urban Terrorism: Theory, Practice, and Response*. New York: Free Press, 1975.

Carlton, David, and Schaerf, Carlo, eds. *International Terrorism and World Security*. London: Croom Helm, 1975.

Carmichael, Joel. *Stalin's Masterpiece*. New York: St. Martin's Press, 1976.

Cleveland, Raymond H., et al. *A Global Perspective on Transnational Terrorism: A Case Study of Libya*. Maxwell Air Force Base, Ala.: Air War College, 1977.

Cline, Ray S. "Terrorism: Seedbed for Soviet Influence." *Midstream*, vol. 26, pp. 5–8. New York: Theodor Herzl Foundation, May 1980.

Clutterbuck, Richard L. *Guerrillas and Terrorists*. London: Faber & Faber, 1977. Athens, Ohio: Ohio University Press, 1980.

————. *Living with Terrorism*. New York: Arlington House, 1975.

————. "Terrorist International." *Army Quarterly and Defense Journal* 104 (January 1974): 154–159.

Conquest, Robert. *The Great Terror: Stalin's Purge of the Thirties*. Harmondsworth: Penguin, 1971.

————. *The Human Cost of Soviet Communism*. Washington, D.C.: GPO, 1970.

Convention to Prevent and Punish the Acts of Terrorism Taking the Form of Crimes Against Persons and Related Extortion That Are of International Significance. Washington, D.C.: GPO, 1971.

Crelinsten, Ronald D. *Terrorism and Criminal Justice*. Lexington, Mass.: Lexington Books, 1978.

Crenshaw, Martha, ed. *Terrorism, Legitimacy, and Power: The Consequences of Political Violence*. Middletown, Conn.: Wesleyan University Press, 1983.

Dallin, Alexander, and Breslauer, George W. *Political Terror in*

Communist Systems. Stanford, Calif.: Stanford University Press, 1970.

Debray, R. *Revolution in the Revolution?* New York: Monthly Review Press, 1967.

————. *Strategy for Revolution*. Harmondsworth: Penguin, 1973.

Dobson, Christopher, and Payne, Ronald. *The Weapons of Terror: International Terrorism at Work*. London: Macmillan & Co., 1979.

Draper, Theodore. *Castro's Revolution: Myths and Realities*. New York: Praeger Publishers, 1962.

Evans, Alona E., and Murphy, John F., eds. *Legal Aspects of International Terrorism*. Lexington, Mass.: Lexington Books, 1978.

Evans, Ernst. *Calling a Truce to Terror: The American Response to International Terrorism*. Westport, Conn.: Greenwood Press, 1979.

Francis, Samuel T. *The Soviet Strategy of Terror*. Washington, D.C.: Heritage Foundation, 1981.

Freedman, Lawrence Zelic, and Alexander, Yonah, eds. *Perspectives on Terrorism*. Wilmington, Del.: Scholarly Resources, 1983.

Friedlander, Robert A. *Terrorism: Documents of International and Local Control*. 2 vols. Dobbs Ferry, N.Y.: Oceana Publications, 1979.

Galula, Davis. *Counterinsurgency Warfare: Theory and Practice*. New York: Praeger Publishers, 1964.

Garthoff, Raymond L. *Soviet Strategy in the Nuclear Age*. London: Allen & Unwin, 1958.

Gaucher, Roland. *The Terrorists: From Tzarist Russia to the O.A.S.* Translated by P. Spurlin. London: Secker & Warburg, 1968.

Gellner, John. *Bayonets in the Streets*. Don Mills, Ont.: Collier-Macmillan Canada, 1974.

Giap, Yo-nguyen. *People's War, People's Army: The Viet Cong Insurrection Manual for Underdeveloped Countries*. New York: Praeger Publishers, 1962.

Goode, Stephen. *Guerrilla Warfare and Terrorism*. New York: F. Watts, 1977.

Gott, Richard. *Guerrilla Movements in Latin America*. London: Thomas Nelson, 1970.

Gross, Feliks. *Violence in Politics: Terror and Political Assassination in Eastern Europe and Russia*. The Hague: Mouton, 1972.

Guevara, Ché. *Reminiscences of the Cuban Revolutionary War*. Translated by V. Ortiz. New York: Monthly Review Press, 1968.

Guevara, Ernesto. *Ché Guevara on Guerrilla Warfare*. Translated by Harries-Clichy Peterson. New York: Praeger Publishers, 1961.

Guevara, Ernesto Ché. *Guerrilla Warfare*. New York: Random House, 1961.

Guillen, Abraham. *Philosophy of the Urban Guerrilla*. Translated by D. C. Hodge. New York: William Morrow & Co., 1973.

Gurr, Ted Robert. *Why Men Rebel*. Princeton: Princeton University Press, 1970.

Halperin, Ernst. *Terrorism in Latin America*. Beverly Hills: Sage Publications, 1975.

Hanning, Hugh, ed. *Soviet Union in Europe and the Near East: Her Capabilities and Intentions*. London: Royal United Service Institution, 1970.

Havens, Murray Clark. *Assassination and Terrorism*. Manchaca, Tex.: S. Swift, 1975.

Heller, Michael. "The Gulag Archipelago and Its Inhabitants." *Survey* 20 (Spring–Summer 1974): 211–227.

Hodges, Donald Clark. *National Liberation Fronts: 1960–1970*. New York: William Morrow & Co., 1972.

Horner, Charles. "The Facts About Terrorism." *Commentary* 69, pp. 40–45. New York: American Jewish Committee, June 1980.

Horrell, Muriel. *Terrorism in Southern Africa*. Johannesburg: South African Institute of Race Relations, 1968.

Hosmer, Stephen T. *Viet Cong Repression and Its Implications for the Future*. Lexington, Mass.: Lexington Books, 1970.

The Human Cost of Communism in Vietnam. Washington, D.C.: GPO, 1970.

The Human Cost of Communism in Vietnam: A Compendium. Washington, D.C.: GPO, 1972.

Hutchinson, Martha Crenshaw. "Transnational Terrorism and World Politics." *Jerusalem Journal of International Relations* 1 (Winter 1975); 109–129.

Hyams, Edward. *Terrorists and Terrorism*. New York: St. Martin's Press, 1974.

Hyman, Anthony. *Afghanistan Under Soviet Domination, 1964–1981*. New York: St. Martin's Press, 1982.

"International Terrorism." *Stanford Journal of International Studies* 12 (Spring 1977).

Jacobson, Carl. *Soviet Strategy—Soviet Foreign Policy*. Glasgow, Scotland: Robert MacLehose, 1972.

Jenkins, Brian M. *The Five Stages of Urban Guerrilla Warfare*. Santa Monica, Calif.: Rand, 1974.

――――. *International Terrorism: A New Mode of Conflict*. Santa Monica, Calif.: Rand, 1974. Los Angeles: Crescent Publications, 1975.

Johnson, Chalmers A. *Revolutionary Change*. Boston: Little, Brown & Co., 1966.

Jordan, Amos A., and Taylor, William J., Jr. *American National Security: Policy and Process*. Baltimore: Johns Hopkins University Press, 1981.

Kautsky, Karl. *Terrorism and Communism: A Contribution to the Natural History of Revolution*. Translated by W. H. Kerridge. London: Allen & Unwin, 1920.

Kitson, Frank. *Low Intensity Operations: Subversion, Insurgency, Peace-Keeping*. London: Faber, 1972.

Kupperman, Robert H., and Trent, D. *Terrorism: Threat, Reality, Response*. Stanford, Calif.: Hoover Institution, 1979.

Laffin, John. *Fedayeen*. New York: Macmillan Co., 1973.

Lambrick, H. T. *The Terrorist*. London: Benn, 1972.

Laqueur, Walter. *Guerrilla: A Historical and Critical Study*. Boston: Little, Brown & Co., 1976.

――――. *Terrorism*. Boston: Little, Brown & Co., 1977.

――――. *The Terrorism Reader: A Historical Anthology*. Philadelphia: Temple University Press, 1978.

Lee, Alfred McClung. *Terrorism in Northern Ireland*. Bayside, N.Y.: General Hall, 1983.

Leiden, C., and Schmitt, K. M. *The Politics of Violence: Revolution in the Modern World*. Englewood Cliffs, N.J.: Prentice-Hall, 1968.

Leites, Nathan, and Wolf, Charles, Jr. *Rebellion and Authority: An Analytical Essay on Insurgent Conflicts*. Chicago: Markham, Lieuwen, Edwin, 1970.

Lenin, V. I. *Imperialism, the Highest Stage of Capitalism*. Moscow: Progress, 1970.

Lewytzkyj, Borys, comp. *The Stalinist Terror in the Thirties: Documentation from the Soviet Press*. Stanford, Calif.: Hoover Institution, 1974.

Livingston, Maurius, ed. *International Terrorism in the Contemporary World*. Westport, Conn.: Greenwood Press, 1978.

Livingstone, Neil C. *The War Against Terrorism*. Lexington, Mass.: Lexington Books, 1983.

Mallin, Jay, ed. *Terror and Urban Guerrillas: A Study of the Tactics and Documents*. Coral Gables, Fla.: University of Miami, 1971.

Mao Tse-tung. *Basic Tactics*. New York: Praeger Publishers, 1966.

————. *On Guerrilla Warfare*. New York: Praeger Publishers, 1961.

Marcuse, Herbert. *Counterrevolution and Revolt*. Boston: Beacon Press, 1972.

Marighella, Carlos. *Minimanual of the Urban Guerrilla*. Havana: Tricontinental, n.d.; London: International Institute for Strategic Studies, 1971.

McKnight, Gerald. *The Mind of the Terrorist*. London: Joseph, 1974.

————. *The Terrorist Mind*. Indianapolis: Bobbs-Merrill, 1974.

Merleau-Ponty, Maurice. *Humanism and Terror: An Essay on the Communist Problem*. Boston: Beacon Press, 1969.

Miller, Aaron David. *The PLO and the Politics of Survival*. Washington Papers, no. 99, vol. 11. Washington, D.C.: Center for Strategic and International Studies, Georgetown University, 1983.

Morris, Michael. *Terrorism*. Cape Town: H. Timmins, 1971.

Moss, Robert. *Urban Guerrillas*. London: Temple Smith, 1972.

————. *The War for the Cities*. New York: Coward, 1972.

Payne, Pierre Stephen Robert. *The Terrorists: The Story of the Forerunners of Stalin*. New York: Funk & Wagnalls Co., 1967.

Pike, Douglas Eugene. *Hanoi's Strategy of Terror*. Bangkok: South-East Asia Treaty Organization, 1970.

Pomeroy, William J. *Guerrilla Warfare and Marxism*. New York: International, 1968.

Possony, Stefan T., and Bouchey, L. Francis. *International Terrorism: The Communist Connection*. Washington, D.C.: American Council for World Freedom, 1978.

Pryce-Jones, David. *The Face of Defeat: Palestinian Refugees and Guerrillas*. London: Weiderfeld & Nicholson, 1972.

Pye, Lucian W., ed. *Guerrilla Communism in Malaya: Its Social and Political Meaning*. Princeton: Princeton University Press, 1956.

Rapoport, David C. *Assassination and Terrorism*. Toronto: Canadian Broadcasting, 1971.

Rapoport, David C., and Alexander, Yonah, eds. *The Morality of Terrorism: Religious and Secular Justifications*. Elmsford, N.Y.: Pergamon Press, 1982.

Schram, Stuart. *The Political Thought of Mao Tse-tung*. London: Pelican, 1969.

Scott, Harriet Fast, ed. *Soviet Military Strategy*. 3d ed. New York: Crane, Russak, 1975.

Sobel, Lester A., ed. *Palestinian Impasse: Arab Guerrillas and International Terror*. New York: Facts on File, 1977.

Solzhenitsyn, Alexander. *The Gulag Archipelago*. New York: Harper & Row, 1973.

Sterling, Claire. *The Terror Network*. New York: Holt, Rinehart & Winston, 1981.

Tanham, George Kilpatrick. *Communist Revolutionary Warfare*. New York: Praeger Publishers, 1961.

Taylor, William J., Jr., and Maaranen, Steven A., eds. *The Future of Conflict in the 1980s*. Lexington, Mass.: Lexington Books, 1983.

Terrorism: An International Journal, vols. 1–6, 1977–1983.

Trotsky, Leon. *Against Individual Terrorism*. New York: Pathfinder, 1974.

United Nations. General Assembly, Ad Hoc Committee on International Terrorism. *Report*. New York: United Nations, 1973.

U.S. Central Intelligence Agency. Directorate of Intelligence. *International Terrorism in 1976*. Washington, D.C.: CIA, 1977, 1978.

U.S. Congress. House. Committee on Foreign Affairs. Subcommittee on the Near East and South East Asia. *International Terrorism*. 93d Cong., 2d sess. Washington, D.C.: GPO, 1974.

U.S. Congress. House. Committee on Internal Security. *The Symbionese Liberation Army*. Washington, D.C.: GPO, 1974.

U.S. Congress. House. Committee on Internal Security. *Terrorism*. Washington, D.C.: GPO, 1974.

U.S. Congress. House. Committee on Public Works and Transportation. Subcommittee on Aviation. *International Terrorism*. 95th Cong., 2d sess. on H.R. 13261. Washington, D.C.: GPO, 1978.

U.S. Congress. Senate. Committee on the Judiciary. Subcommittee on Security and Terrorism. *The Role of Cuba in International Terrorism and Subversion*. 97th Cong., 2d sess. Washington, D.C.: GPO, 1982.

U.S. Congress. Senate. Committee on the Judiciary. Subcommittee on Security and Terrorism. *The Role of the Soviet Union, Cuba, and East Germany in Fomenting Terrorism in Southern Africa*. 97th Cong., 2d sess., vols. 1 and 2. Washington, D.C.: GPO, 1982.

U.S. Congress. Senate. Committee on the Judiciary. Subcommittee on Security and Terrorism. *Soviet, East German, and Cuban Involvement in Fomenting Terrorism in Southern Africa*. 97th Cong., 2d sess. Washington, D.C.: GPO, 1982.

U.S. Congress. Senate. Committee on the Judiciary. Subcommittee on

Security and Terrorism. *Terrorism: Origins, Direction, and Support.* 97th Cong., 1st sess. Washington, D.C.: GPO, 1981.

U.S. Congress. Senate. Committee on the Judiciary. Subcommittee on Security and Terrorism. *Terrorism: The Turkish Experience.* 97th Cong. 1st sess. Washington, D.C.: GPO, 1981.

U.S. Congress. Senate. Committee on the Judiciary. Subcommittee to Investigate the Administration of the Internal Security Act and Other Internal Security Laws. *Trotskyite Terrorist International.* 94th Cong. 1st sess., July 24, 1975. Washington, D.C.: GPO, 1975.

Walter, Eugene Victor. *Terror and Resistance.* New York: Oxford, 1969; London/New York: Oxford, 1972.

Wardlaw, Grant. *Political Terrorism: Political Tactics and Counter Measures.* New York: Cambridge University Press, 1983.

Watson, Francis M. *Political Terrorism: The Threat and the Response.* Washington, D.C.: R. B. Luce, 1976.

Waugh, William, L., Jr. *International Terrorism: How Nations Respond to Terrorists.* Salisbury, N.C.: Documentary Publications, 1982.

Weeks, Albert L., and Bodie, William C., eds. *War and Peace: Soviet Russia Speaks.* New York: National Strategy Information Center, 1983.

Wilkinson, Paul. *Political Terrorism.* London: Macmillan & Co., 1974; New York: Wiley, 1975.

———. *Political Terrorism and the Liberal State.* New York: John Wiley & Sons, 1977.

———. *Terrorism and the Liberal State.* New York: John Wiley & Sons, 1979.

Index

Fermaershi, Fateh Mohammad (Gen.), 25
Ford, Gerald (Pres.), 71
Forgan "terrorists," 25
Franceschini, Alberto, 59

Gemayel, Bashir, 38
Green Berets, 26
Grinevsky, Oleg A., 35, 83–105
Gromyko, Andrei, 35, 36, 50, 83–106
GRU. *See* Soviet Military Intelligence
Guevara, Ana Maria, 71
Guevara, Ché, 71

Habash, George, 35, 40, 49, 83
Habib, Philip, 51
Haddad, Wadi (Dr.), 58
Haig, Alexander, 20, 21
Harakat Tahrir Falastin, 32
Harris, Abdel, 63
Hlapane, Bartholomew, 62
Ho Chi Minh, 11
Hussein I (King), 64

International Department of the Popular Front. *See* Popular Front for the Liberation of Palestine (PFLP)
Iranian Freedom Fighters, 67
Irish Republican Army (IRA), 7, 57, 59, 64, 69, 70
Italian intelligence. *See* SID
Iyad, Abu, 39–42, 44, 51, 134

Jaber, Adnan, 47
Japanese Red Army (URA), 58, 61, 63, 64
Jibril, Ahmed, 33, 35, 66, 83
Jihad, Abu, 44, 51, 134
John Paul II (Pope), 7, 28, 29, 60, 75, 144
Johnson, Lyndon (Pres.), 77

Kabah, Taisir, 83
Kaddoumi, Farouk, 34, 36, 41
Kahwaji, Habib, 83
Kaunda, Kenneth, 25
Kennedy, John F. (Pres.), 11, 27, 77, 78
KGB. *See* Soviet Security Agency
Khrushchev, Nikita, 10–12, 16, 56, 73
Konkret, 58
Kosygin, Alexei, 35
Kotschergine, Wadim, 71

Lenin, V. I., 9, 10, 12, 75
Lenin Institute, 56
Letelier, Orlando, 28
Liberation Movement Department of the Popular Front. *See* Popular Front for the Liberation of Palestine (PFLP)
Lumumba, Patrice, 11, 23, 56, 58

Madani, Ayatollah A., 25
Mahmoud, Zaiden Uni, 44
Mandela, Nelson, 61
Mao Tse-tung, 76
Mawahdi, Ahmed, 45
Mazin, Abu, 41
Meinhof, Ulrike, 16, 58. *See also* Baader-Meinhof Gang
Meizer, Abed El Mahsin Abu, 83
Miceli, Vito, 59
Mordbinov, Vladimir, 68
Moro, Aldo, 60, 144
Moss, Robert, 29
Movement of the Revolutionary Left (MLR), 56, 71
Musa, Abu, 32

Nabris, Bashad Ahmed Abdul Aziz an-, 48
Naji, Tlal, 83
Nasrat ul-Hakh, 13
Nasser, Gamal 'Abdul, 32, 35
National Liberation Front (FLN), 11
National Social Party, 14
NATO, 6, 7, 21, 42, 144
Nixon, Richard (Pres.), 77
Nujoma, Sam, 61

Operation Litani, 47
Operation Peace for Galilee, 47, 48
Organized Autonomy Movement, 63
Orwell, George, 1, 2

Palestine Liberation Army (PLA), 31, 46, 50, 107, 112
Palestine Liberation Front, 16, 108, 113
Palestine Liberation Organization (PLO), 7, 20, 21, 30–36, 34–41, 43–54, 56, 62, 64, 65, 68, 77, 127, 136, 137
Palestine National Council, 37, 68
Palestinian National Charter, 33